MINECRAFT

MOJANG

KT-438-401

EGMONT

We bring stories to life

First published in Great Britain 2016 by Egmont UK Limited
The Yellow Building, 1 Nicholas Road
London W11 4AN

Written by Craig Jelley
Designed by Joe Bolder, Ryan Marsh and Martin Johansson/Mojang AB.
Illustrations by Joe Bolder and Ryan Marsh.
Production by Louis Harvey.
Special thanks to Lydia Winters, Owen Hill, Markus Toivonen,
Martin Johansson, Marsh Davies and Jesper Öqvist.

A big thank you to all of our testers: Adam Rayment, Alex Gibberd, Alexander Parker,
Bailey Whitehead Browne, Cormac Gilmore, Daniel Scott Phillips, Eden Kneale, Emma Verghese,
Ethan Wilson, Fred Fox, Grace Noble, Isaac Riordan, Jack Dillon, Jack Moody, Jackson Givens,
Jane Simmons, Joseph Sneddon, Marco Kahlhamer, Miranda Ryan-White, Molly Ellerbeck,
Noah Killeen, Oliver Berridge, Oscar Riordan, Robert Simmons, Sami Fyfe, Skye Ingram,
Theo Smith, Thomas Dillon, Thomas Hone, Wilfred Weston.

© 2016 Mojang AB and Mojang Synergies AB. MINECRAFT is a trademark or registered trademark
of Mojang Synergies AB.

All rights reserved.

☐MOJANG

ISBN 978 1 4052 8417 2
63986/1
Printed in Italy

MIX
Paper from
responsible sources
FSC® C018306

Egmont is passionate about helping to preserve the world's remaining ancient forests.
We only use paper from legal and sustainable forest sources.

This book is made from paper certified by the Forest Stewardship Council® (FSC®),
an organisation dedicated to promoting responsible management of forest resources.
For more information on the FSC please visit www.fsc.org. To learn more about
Egmont's sustainable paper policy, please visit www.egmont.co.uk/ethical

ONLINE SAFETY FOR YOUNGER FANS

Spending time online is great fun! Here are a few simple rules to help younger fans stay safe and keep the
internet a great place to spend time:

- Never give out your real name – don't use it as your username.
- Never give out any of your personal details.
- Never tell anybody which school you go to or how old you are.
- Never tell anybody your password except a parent or a guardian.
- Be aware that you must be 13 or over to create an account on many sites. Always check the site policy and
ask a parent or guardian for permission before registering.
- Always tell a parent or guardian if something is worrying you.

Stay safe online. Any website addresses listed in this book are correct at the time of going to print.
However, Egmont is not responsible for content hosted by third parties. Please be aware that online
content can be subject to change and websites can contain content that is unsuitable for children. We
advise that all children are supervised when using the internet.

The publishers have used every endeavour to trace copyright owners and secure appropriate
permissions for materials reproduced in this book. In case of any unintentional omission,
the publishers will be pleased to hear from the relevant copyright owner.

MINECRAFT
™
◪MOJANG

MEDIEVAL FORTRESS

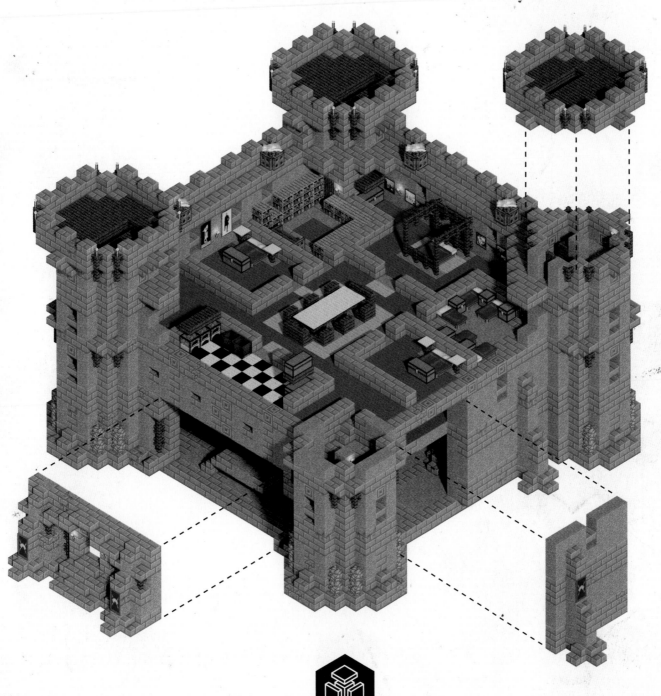

EXPLODED
BUILDS

CONTENTS

◆ Castle

◆ Village

◆ Traps

FORTRESS LAYOUT

The layout of your kingdom is almost as important as the buildings in it. Below is a map of an example kingdom to use as a guide, with page references for each of the builds. Build your castle on high ground to give you an advantage over attackers.

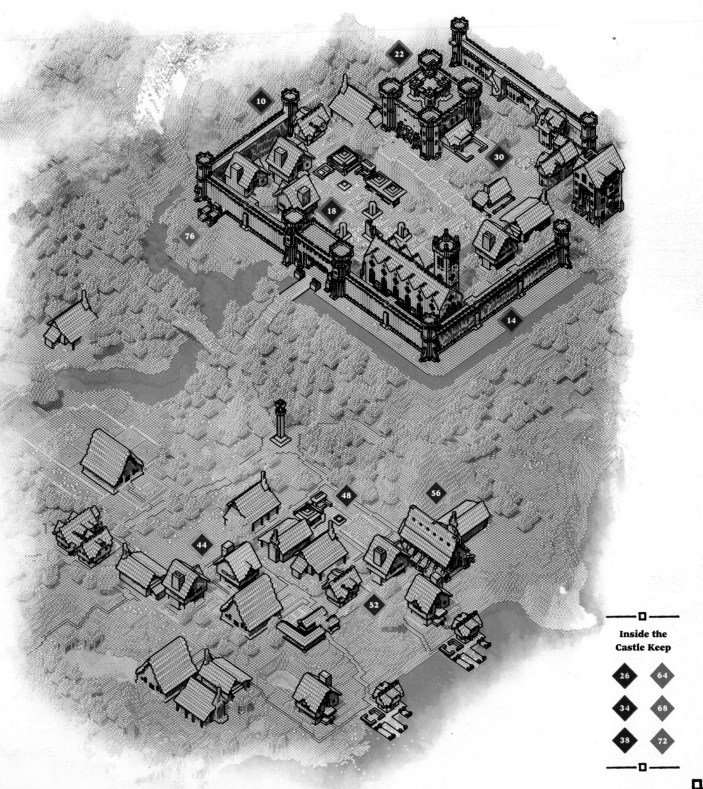

Inside the
Castle Keep

26   64

34   68

38   72

INTRODUCTION

Welcome to Exploded Builds: Medieval Fortress, a book that will teach you how to build your own incredible kingdom. An exploded diagram is provided for each build, which takes the pieces apart to show exactly how to put the build together, and there are clever variants and additions that you can mix and match to make your kingdom.

By the end of this book, you'll have your own unique medieval empire to rule over. You will have constructed an impenetrable castle with fortified walls, towering turrets and a grand throne room to govern from. There will be a bustling village of your own creation surrounding the castle grounds, complete with a busy market, quaint houses and a lively tavern. All of this will be protected by your ingeniously engineered traps, set and ready to spring on uninvited invaders.

There are lots of helpful features in the book, so before you start to design your medieval fortress, take a look at the key below to help you understand the exploded diagrams.

Dimension Lines

The dimension lines show the size of the build, or a section of a build. These are measured by the number of blocks.

Yellow Stained Clay

These blocks are used to improve the visibility of redstone. You can use another type of block when creating the builds.

Connection Lines

These dashed lines show how the different sections will be assembled and show exactly where blocks should fit together.

Blueprints

These are scattered throughout the book to show the arrangement of blocks and builds that are too big or complicated to show at full size.

Break Line

The break line is used to show the gap between different elements of a build and how far apart they should be.

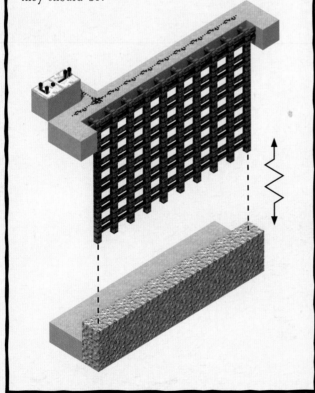

Adjacency Lines

Some blocks have a single edge touching other blocks. These lines show where they meet. You can add an extra block to place blocks that only share a single edge, then destroy the extra block once you're finished.

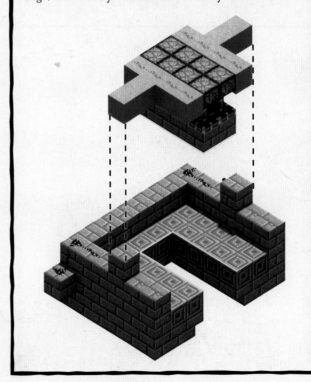

CASTLE

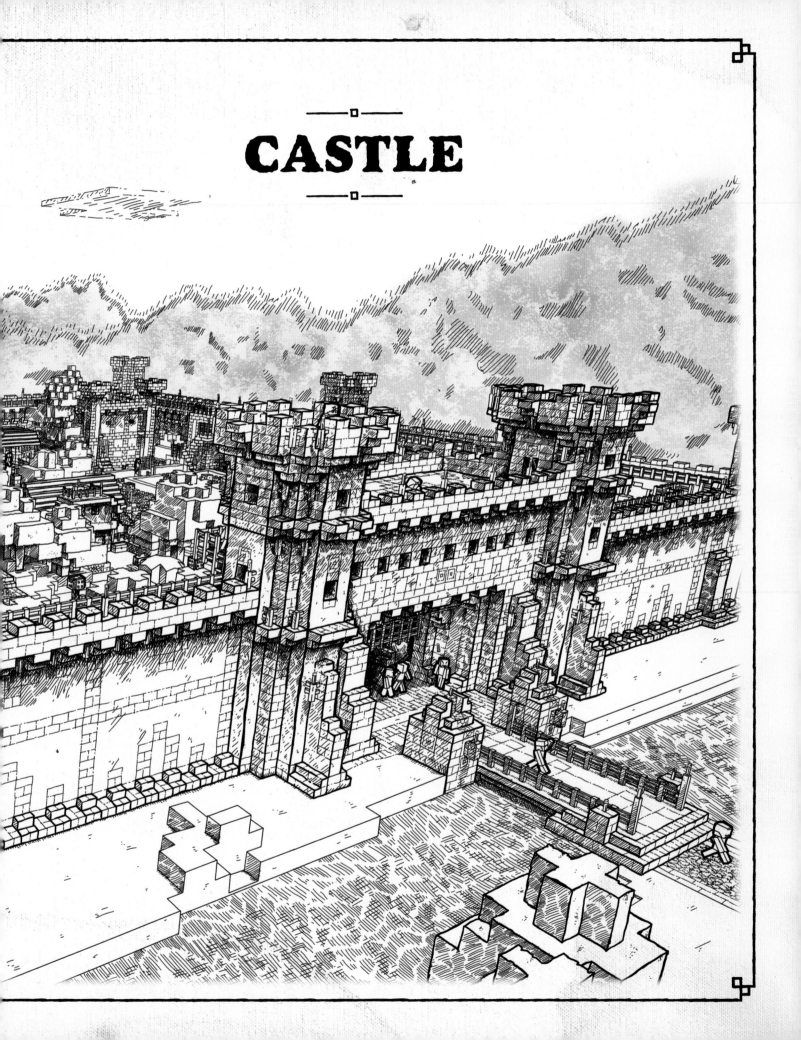

TURRET

⏱ **0.5 HOURS** ❶ ② ③ ④ **BEGINNER**

To keep creepers, zombies and marauding enemies away from your castle, you'll need to see them coming. The first blocks you place in your fortress will become the turrets – made from brick blocks, they will allow you to watch over a wider area, and see enemies in the distance. Add turrets where two walls meet at the corners of your fortress, so you can view the whole kingdom.

Turrets were types of towers that extended above the castle walls, or were built on top of other, larger towers.

Turrets and other castle structures had arrow loops – small, thin openings that allowed archers to shoot at attackers whilst remaining mostly protected.

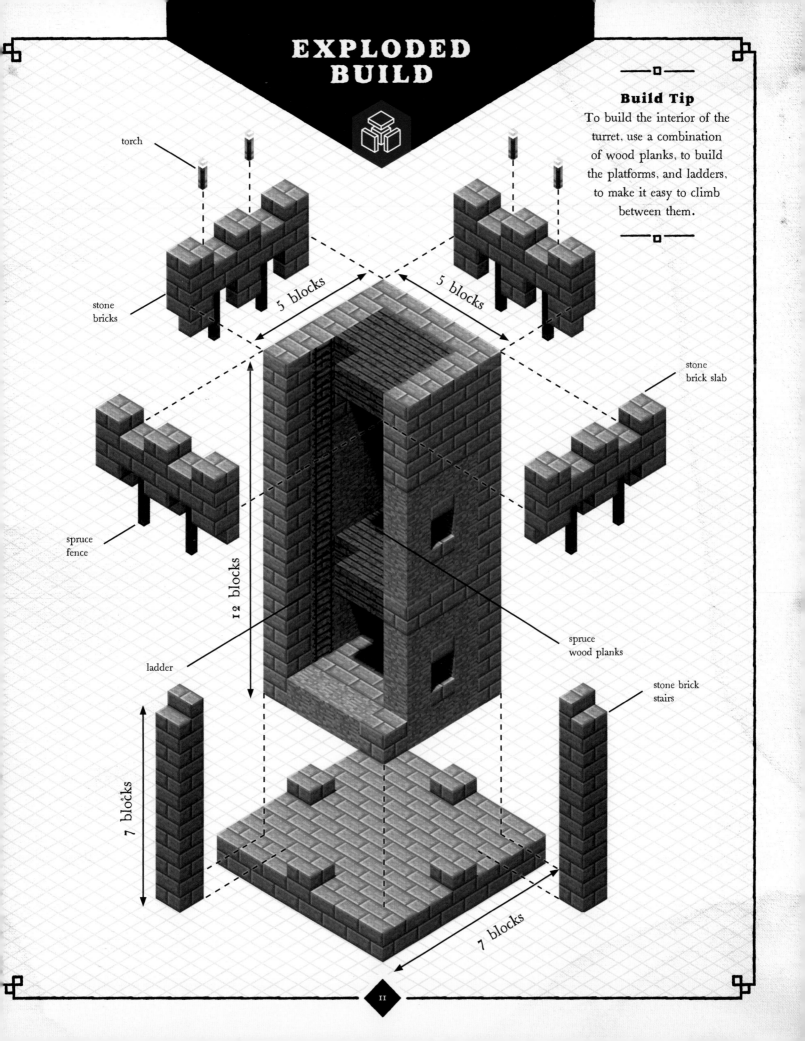

EXPLODED BUILD

Build Tip

To build the interior of the turret, use a combination of wood planks, to build the platforms, and ladders, to make it easy to climb between them.

torch

stone bricks

stone brick slab

spruce fence

12 blocks

ladder

spruce wood planks

stone brick stairs

5 blocks

5 blocks

7 blocks

7 blocks

MIX IT UP

Now you've constructed your basic turrets, it's time to get creative and customise them. You can change the type of blocks you use, the shape of the turrets, and add lots of features to make them unique. You could even have a different style of turret at every corner of your castle walls.

Use obsidian blocks for the floor of the turret as well, otherwise invaders will be able to tunnel in from below.

i Super-strong Walls

To create a stronger turret, swap the weak stone bricks of the walls with obsidian. It's the strongest usable block in the world and has the highest blast resistance, so it can easily withstand creeper explosions and TNT attacks.

There are no obsidian slabs or stairs, so the stone brick ones will have to be kept.

Add cobblestone wall blocks to the top edge of the turret, so soldiers don't fall off.

i Turret Roof

Add a handy roof to the turret. It doesn't matter how tall or what shape it is, but it will limit the target area for attackers to hit patrolling guards, and the less chance they have of being hit, the easier it is for them to stay alive and defend the castle.

Create a shooting platform from which to attack oncoming invaders.

The same style of decoration can be applied to the sides and tops of the rounded turrets.

Redstone torches are dimmer and less visible to attackers.

Rounded Base

Square-based turrets are fine, but for a change of style, try a rounded base. Rounded turrets allow a 360-degree view of the land around the castle, so enemies can be spotted coming from all directions.

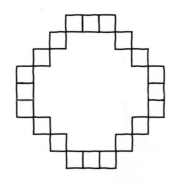

Arrange blocks on the ground in this pattern, then build upwards to make a round turret.

Wooden Theme

Replace the stone decorations around the turret with wood blocks to give it a more varied, rustic look. All stone blocks have wooden alternatives so every block can be swapped to create a different style.

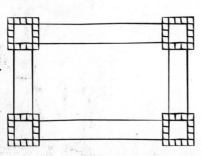

Place turrets where two walls meet, as shown below. They can be added either side of the portcullis as guard towers too.

Stack the wooden blocks on top of each other, rather than attaching to the wall, so that they form one continuous wooden beam.

OUTER WALL

⏱ **1.5 HOURS** ❶❷③④ **EASY**

Now you've got the turrets in place, it's time to build the fortifications. Every structure you build will be within this outer wall, so make sure that it's large enough. The wall will be your first line of defence against outsiders, so it needs to be made from durable blocks. You might need to destroy part of the wall to build turrets later on, but the most important thing is to get the size and shape of your fortress correct.

The walking area on top of the outer wall was sheltered by the parapet, the raised edge of the wall, which protected anyone roaming along the walls from harm.

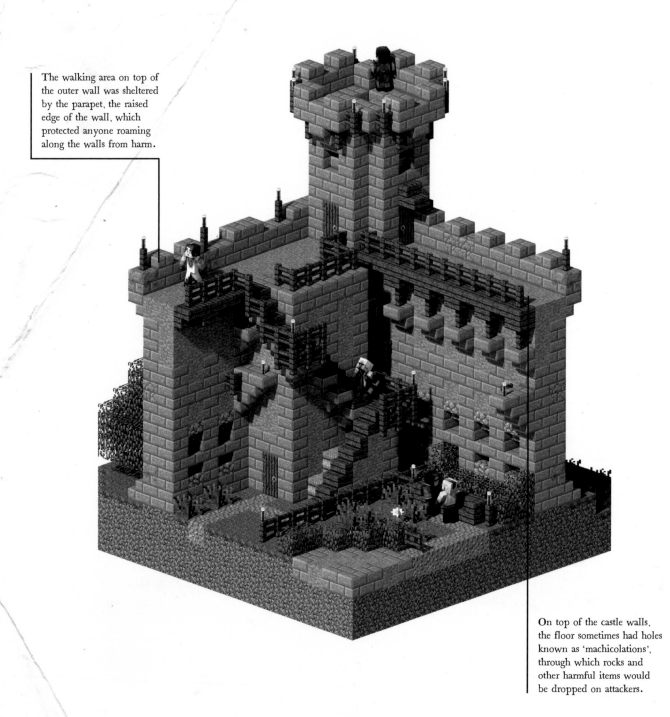

On top of the castle walls, the floor sometimes had holes known as 'machicolations', through which rocks and other harmful items would be dropped on attackers.

◆ 14

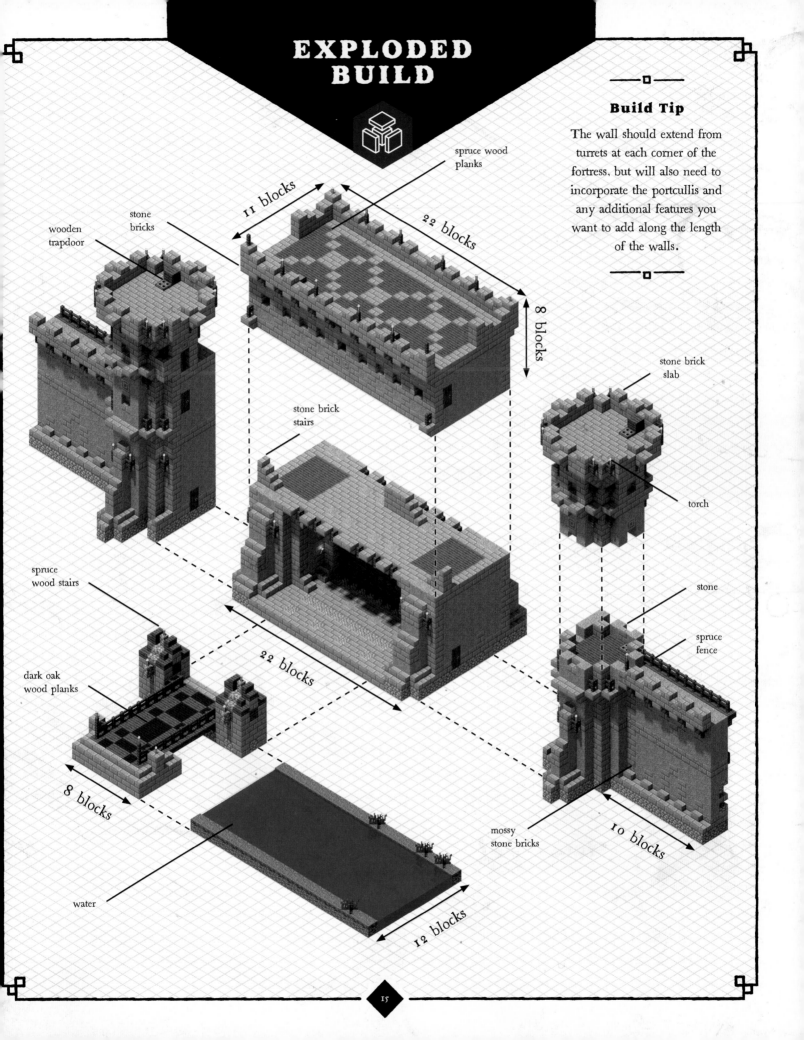

EXPLODED BUILD

spruce wood planks

wooden trapdoor

stone bricks

11 blocks

22 blocks

8 blocks

Build Tip

The wall should extend from turrets at each corner of the fortress, but will also need to incorporate the portcullis and any additional features you want to add along the length of the walls.

stone brick slab

stone brick stairs

torch

spruce wood stairs

dark oak wood planks

22 blocks

stone

spruce fence

8 blocks

water

mossy stone bricks

10 blocks

12 blocks

MIX IT UP

The simple walls you have surrounded your fortress with are tall enough to keep intruders out, however, they're a bit plain. With these few simple additions, your walls can become a defensive masterpiece. Introducing moats and drawbridges can cause problems for invaders too.

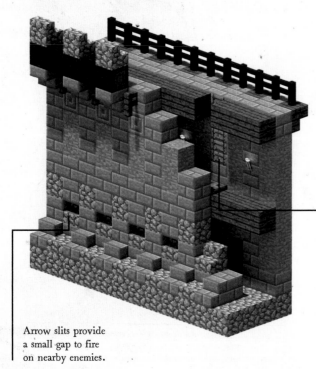

Inner Walls

If the fortress is under siege then troops need to be able to navigate the castle walls quickly. Paths in the interior of the walls allow soldiers to reach a different defence point whilst avoiding the threat of arrows and large siege weapons like catapults.

Ladders placed every few blocks make it easier to get to the top of the wall.

Arrow slits provide a small gap to fire on nearby enemies.

Indestructible Defences

A combination of obsidian and water can be used to create this ultimate wall. The blast resistance of the obsidian will render TNT attacks useless, while the water stops invaders from mining it away and breaking through.

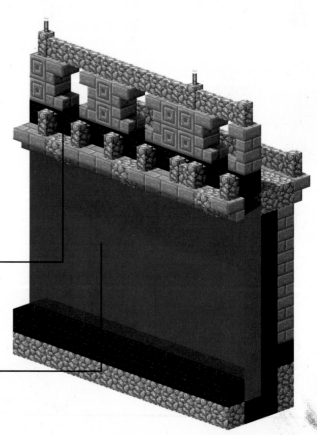

Larger styles of crenellations like this one can be used to increase defence, but reduce scope.

Fortress Facts

The top of the castle walls had crenellations – raised 'merlons' that provided defence, and the gaps, or 'crenels', which soldiers could shoot through.

The water source blocks should be surrounded by obsidian so invaders can't swim over the wall.

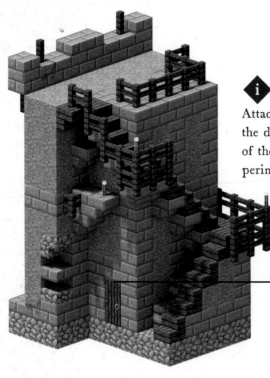

◆ Wall Access

Attackers can strike at any time. If scouts spot anyone in the distance, it's important that forces can reach the top of the walls quickly. Simple staircases along the inside perimeter of the wall reduce the time it takes archers to reach the battlements.

Add doors by the stairs so soldiers have the option to enter the interior of the wall, or climb to the top of it.

Drawbridges should be made from stone blocks. Wooden blocks may burn over lava or netherrack moats.

◆ Deadly Moats

Water moats are more of an inconvenience than a defence. However, if the water is swapped for lava, cactus or netherrack then attackers will have to take damage before they can reach the wall.

A working drawbridge can be created using the same system as the portcullis on page 18.

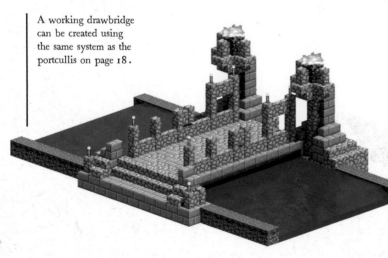

◆ Drawbridge Styles

Not everyone who visits the castle will be trying to get their hands on stashes of treasure, so it's important to provide a friendly welcome for guests. As the first thing visitors will see of the castle, drawbridges should be extravagant and impressive.

PORTCULLIS

⏱ **2 HOURS** ❶❷❸❹ **EXPERIENCED**

Along with the drawbridge, the portcullis was the main feature that kept unwanted people out of a medieval castle. The heavy gate was controlled by a pulley system and operated by guards at the gatehouse, who would judge whether visitors were allowed in. With this build, you can replicate the pulley system with redstone, pistons and gravel, so you can control who can enter your fortress too.

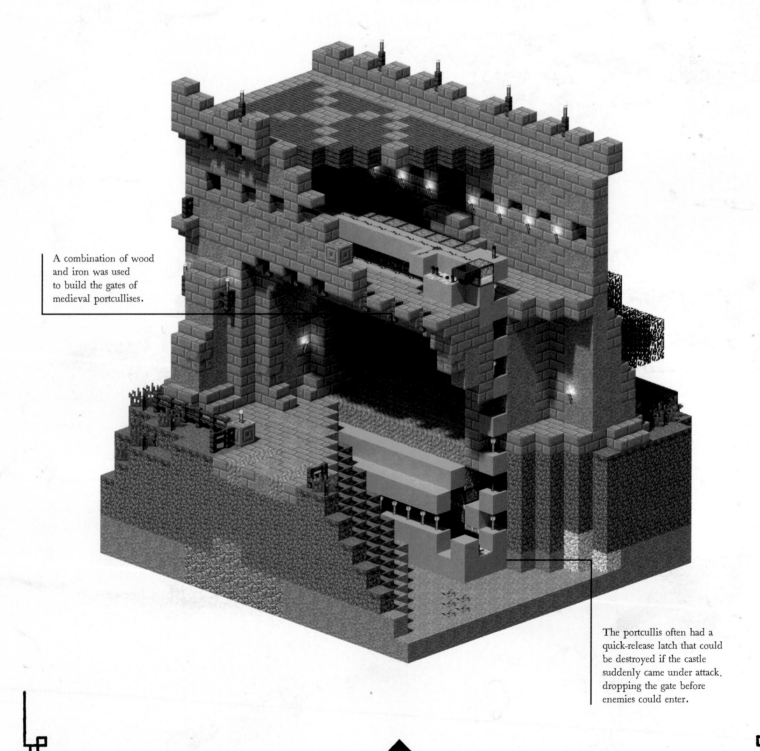

A combination of wood and iron was used to build the gates of medieval portcullises.

The portcullis often had a quick-release latch that could be destroyed if the castle suddenly came under attack, dropping the gate before enemies could enter.

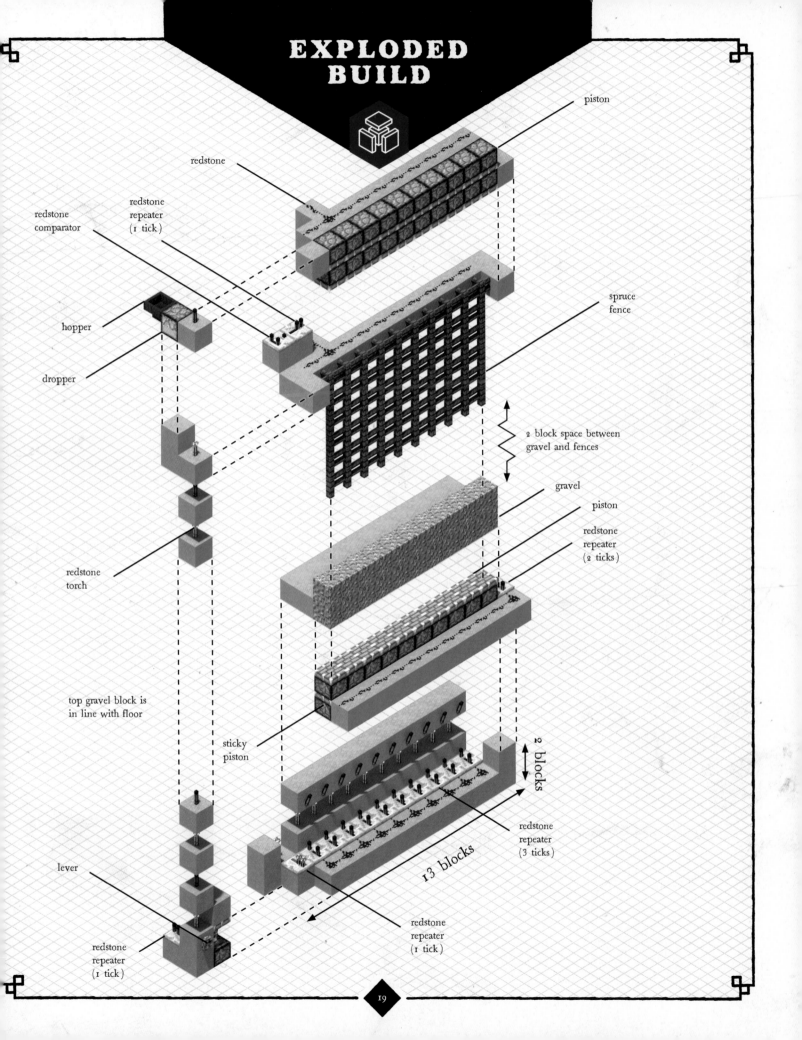

piston

redstone

redstone comparator

redstone repeater (1 tick)

hopper

dropper

spruce fence

2 block space between gravel and fences

redstone torch

gravel

piston

redstone repeater (2 ticks)

top gravel block is in line with floor

sticky piston

2 blocks

lever

redstone repeater (3 ticks)

13 blocks

redstone repeater (1 tick)

redstone repeater (1 tick)

GETTING IT RIGHT

The portcullis relies on two opposing mechanisms; one that pushes the gate up, and one that pushes it back down again. Both of these mechanisms rely on gravel blocks, which fall when nothing is underneath them, and a series of redstone torches.

① Dual Sequence

The lower portcullis mechanism is powered by two sequences of redstone controlled by the pull of a lever. The sequence at the front consists of redstone and redstone repeaters, which power the row of sticky pistons. The back sequence triggers an alternating pattern of redstone torches, which then power the pistons above the sticky pistons. Together, these sequences push the gravel blocks up two spaces.

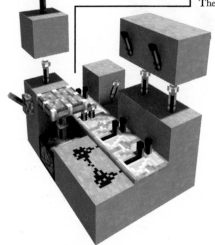

The block on top of the sticky piston has been removed to show the redstone torch.

② Power Up

When the lever is pulled again, the redstone charge ascends up a column of redstone torches to the mechanism that controls the top rows of pistons. The second pull of the lever means that the bottom redstone torch is off, and the top torch is on, powering the 'engine' of the portcullis.

A stack of dirt will power the hopper just as well as a stack of redstone. Make sure that the hopper is attached directly to the front of the dropper.

③ Feeding the Machine

The redstone current will finally reach the top and power a dropper, which will spit out an item into a hopper. The hopper in turn powers a redstone comparator, which feeds through a redstone repeater and across another dual redstone series – this one powers the top two rows of downward-facing pistons.

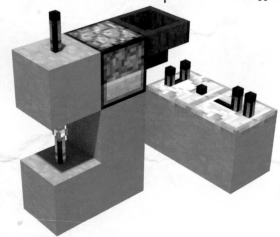

4 ◆ Open and Close

The main mechanisms are now in place. On the first pull of the lever, the bottom pistons will push the gravel and fence blocks up, leaving a gap of two blocks - just enough for a player to fit through. When the lever is pulled again, the top pistons will push the same blocks back down, closing the gap.

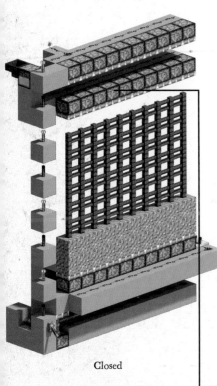

Closed

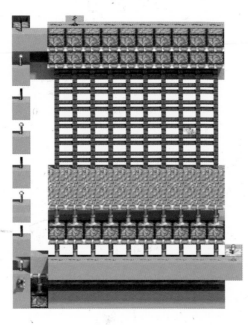

Opening

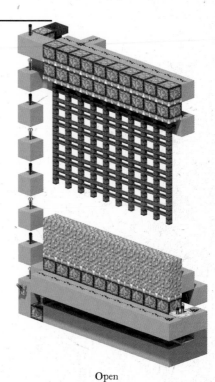

Open

When the portcullis is down there will be a one-block gap between the top two rows of pistons.

The hopper should be placed directly on the dropper, otherwise the fuel will fall to the ground.

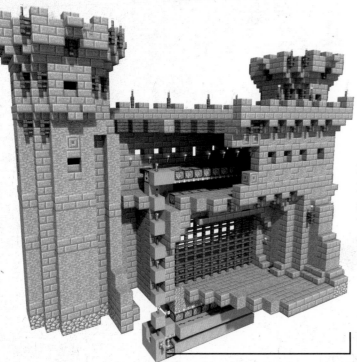

5 ◆ Putting it Together

Now the portcullis is working, it should be concealed. It should fit into a 14 block-wide area of the wall, with the foundations started in a 14 x 3 block-deep hole. The gravel blocks should align horizontally with the floor level and be closer to the inside of the walls. The mechanisms should be disguised within walls and turrets.

A secret underground room can hide the portcullis controls from all but a trusted few.

CASTLE KEEP

⏱ **4 HOURS** ❶❷❸④ **INTERMEDIATE**

Now it's time to build the centrepiece of your fortress – the castle itself. This will be your home as the ruler of the fortress and the citadel within it. The castle will feature the room builds in the following sections and can be used to house the rest of your medieval clan.

The battlement was the walking area atop the castle. It could cover the entire area, or just the perimeter.

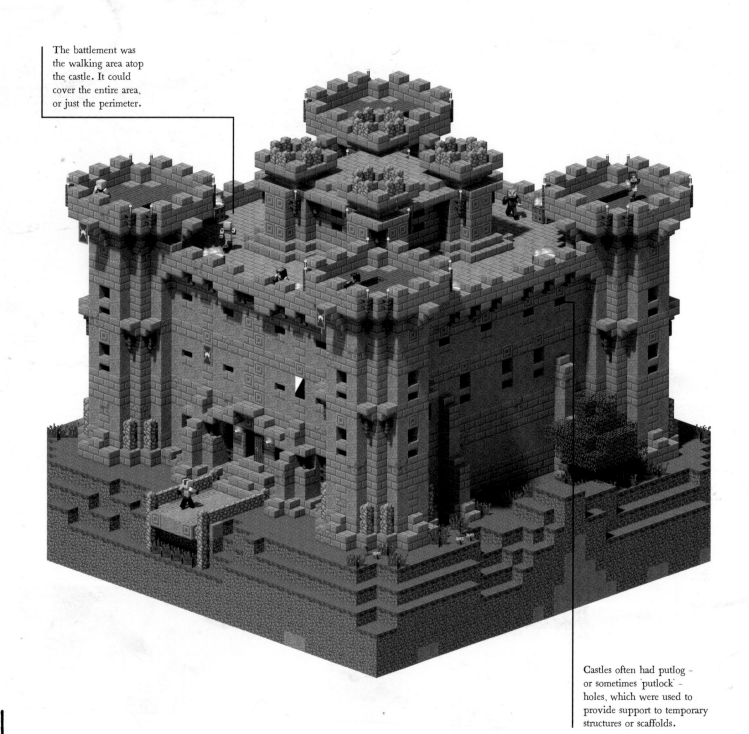

Castles often had putlog – or sometimes 'putlock' – holes, which were used to provide support to temporary structures or scaffolds.

EXPLODED BUILD

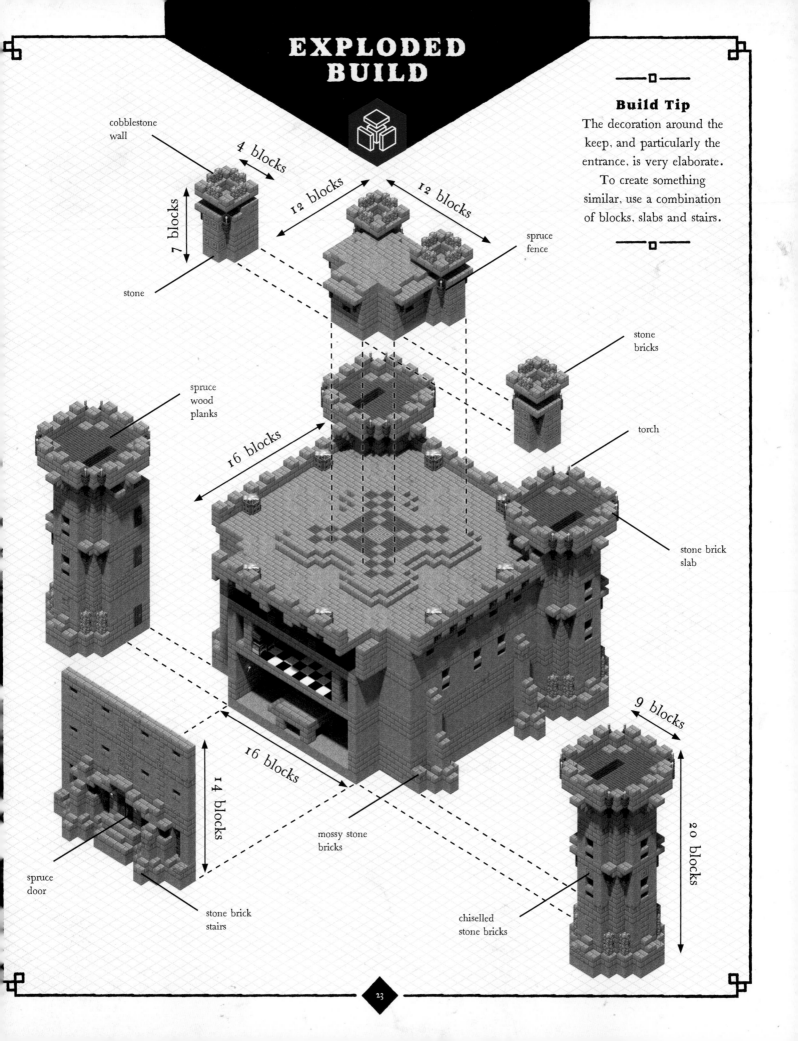

Build Tip

The decoration around the keep, and particularly the entrance, is very elaborate. To create something similar, use a combination of blocks, slabs and stairs.

cobblestone wall

4 blocks

7 blocks

12 blocks

12 blocks

stone

spruce fence

stone bricks

spruce wood planks

torch

16 blocks

stone brick slab

14 blocks

16 blocks

9 blocks

20 blocks

spruce door

mossy stone bricks

chiselled stone bricks

stone brick stairs

MIX IT UP

The keep is the central building in your empire – take inspiration from medieval kings and queens and create a castle that really commands attention and impresses visitors. Use the following tips as a starting point to make your keep completely unique.

ⓘ Germanic Style

Build the castle keep into dramatic scenery like dense forest or at the peak of a huge mountain to give it a fairy-tale appearance. Use tall spires, towers topped with wooden stairs and other similar features to complete the effect.

Lots of towers placed at different heights and in all shapes and sizes form the various levels.

Create T N T cannons using obsidian, water, redstone, redstone repeaters and, of course, T N T.

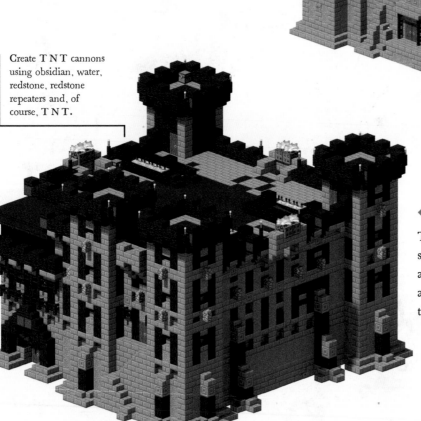

ⓘ Defences

The keep is the last line of defence in a kingdom, so it needs to be well equipped to cope with anyone who breaches the outer walls. Turrets and a sentry lookout will allow surveillance of the immediate area, beacons can signal outposts further afield, while TNT cannons can blow up invading hordes trying to get into the keep.

◆ Room Placement

To finish the castle keep, the room layout will need to be planned. Some of the rooms are discussed in more detail on the following pages - the throne room, dungeon, and enchanting room - but the rest of the castle can be completed with any mixture of rooms. There could be a royal bedchamber, a cavernous hall for throwing feasts, or even a tactical room to plan battles in. The image below shows an example of just one floor, but as many floors as required can be added.

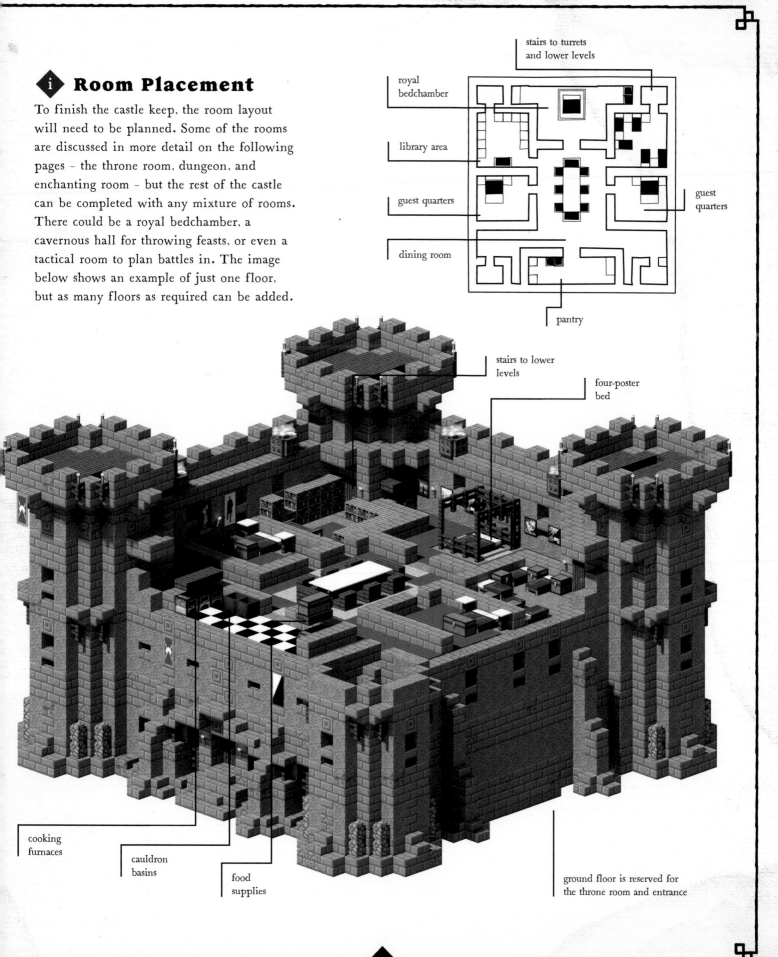

royal bedchamber

stairs to turrets and lower levels

library area

guest quarters

dining room

guest quarters

pantry

stairs to lower levels

four-poster bed

cooking furnaces

cauldron basins

food supplies

ground floor is reserved for the throne room and entrance

THRONE ROOM

⏱ **0.5 HOURS** ❶②③④ **BEGINNER**

Every good king or queen needs a throne room from which to rule over their stronghold and this one should be no different. Whether there are raids on an ore-rich cave to plan, or preparations needed to fend off the latest wave of invaders, the throne room is the perfect place to conduct official business.

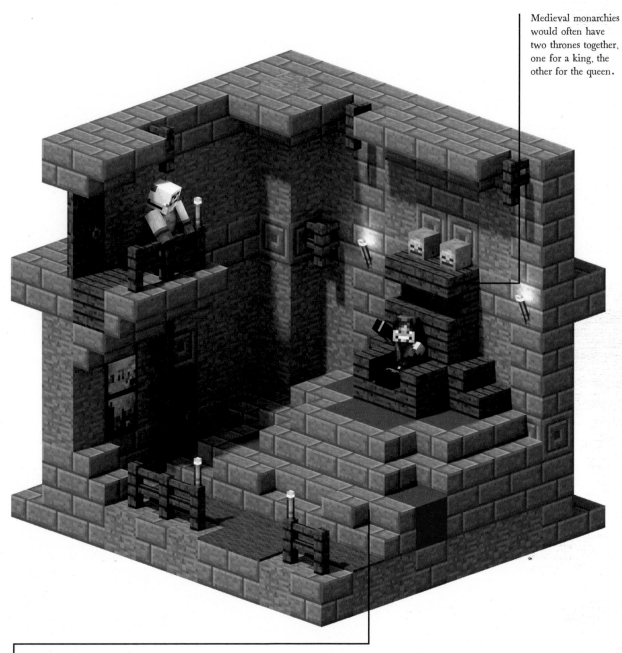

Medieval monarchies would often have two thrones together, one for a king, the other for the queen.

The thrones were often situated on plinths to raise the rulers above everyone else in the room.

EXPLODED BUILD

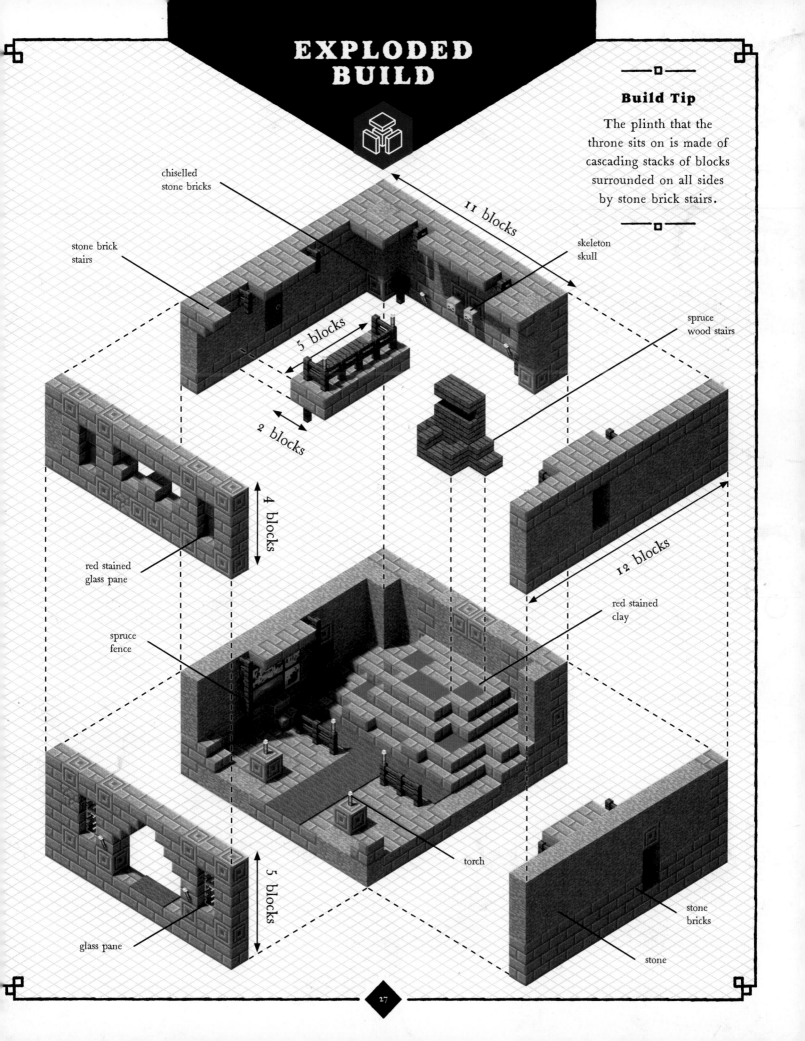

Build Tip

The plinth that the throne sits on is made of cascading stacks of blocks surrounded on all sides by stone brick stairs.

chiselled stone bricks

stone brick stairs

11 blocks

skeleton skull

spruce wood stairs

5 blocks

2 blocks

4 blocks

red stained glass pane

12 blocks

red stained clay

spruce fence

torch

stone bricks

5 blocks

glass pane

stone

27

MIX IT UP

This room is the most symbolically important in the castle, so it should represent everything that your reign stands for. It can feature ostentatious decorations, a tactical base, or a place to meet your loyal subjects. Have a look at these ideas and adapt your throne room accordingly.

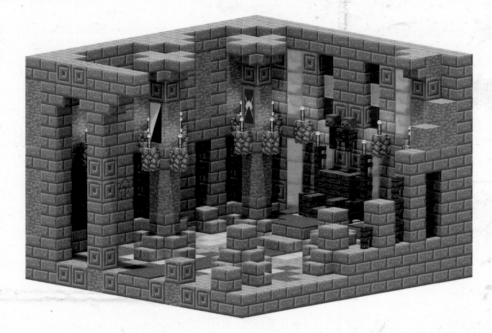

Ornamentation

This room is the one place in the castle that should be as decadent as possible, to show off the riches of the kingdom. Decor such as banners, statues and stained-glass windows can make the room fit for royalty.

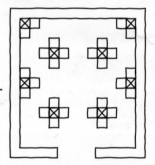

High ceilings should be supported by tall, sturdy pillars. Place them in the throne room according to this plan.

War Room

Make the throne room the seat of power with the addition of a strategy table for the royal guard. From here raids can be planned, sieges thwarted and victories celebrated. The room could even double as a makeshift banquet hall for hosting guests and friendly clans.

A strategy table can be created with activated pistons. They should be placed on redstone torches buried in the floor.

Royal Court

The power of the monarchy will be wielded in the royal court; laws will be passed, taxes collected, and disputes settled. Royalty can survey from a balcony, order-around entourages and pass judgment on the feuds of loyal subjects.

The pleading platform is where members of the public can submit requests to their ruler.

The Royal Seat

The throne is the most important part of the room, and it's where a king or queen will spend most of the day. Gold blocks will make the seat of power stand out and other imaginative features like a personal moat will reinforce the ruler's importance.

Dim redstone torches and lava give the throne room a menacing air.

 ## Infernal Throne

Not every monarch will be kind and benevolent. If the kingdom is to be ruled over with an iron fist then a daunting throne like this one will strike fear into anyone unlucky enough to be brought before their ruler.

BARRACKS

🕐 **1 HOUR**　❶❷③④　**EASY**

With a huge clan following you, you'll need to make sure they can survive the world outside of your fortress. The barracks is the best place to train with your friends and store armour and weapons, so you can easily fend off encroaching spiders, zombies and invaders.

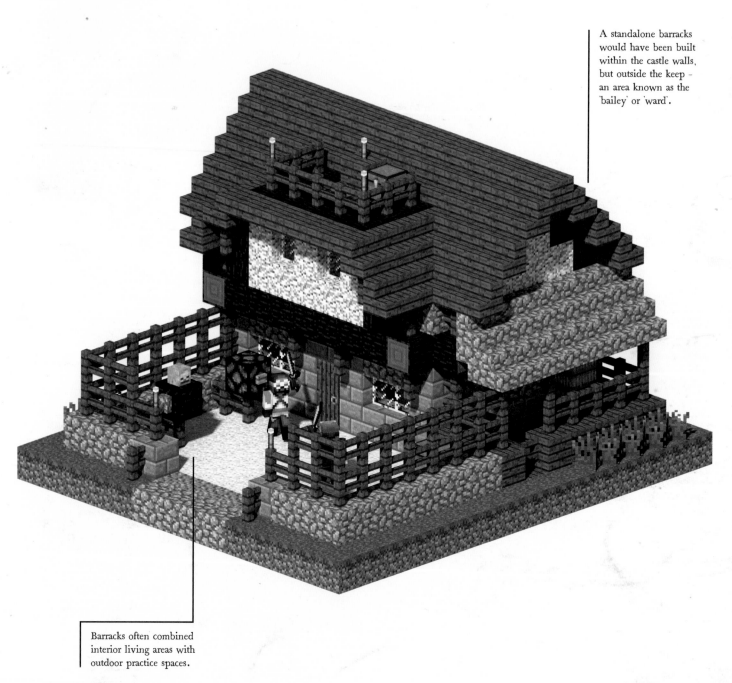

A standalone barracks would have been built within the castle walls, but outside the keep – an area known as the 'bailey' or 'ward'.

Barracks often combined interior living areas with outdoor practice spaces.

EXPLODED BUILD

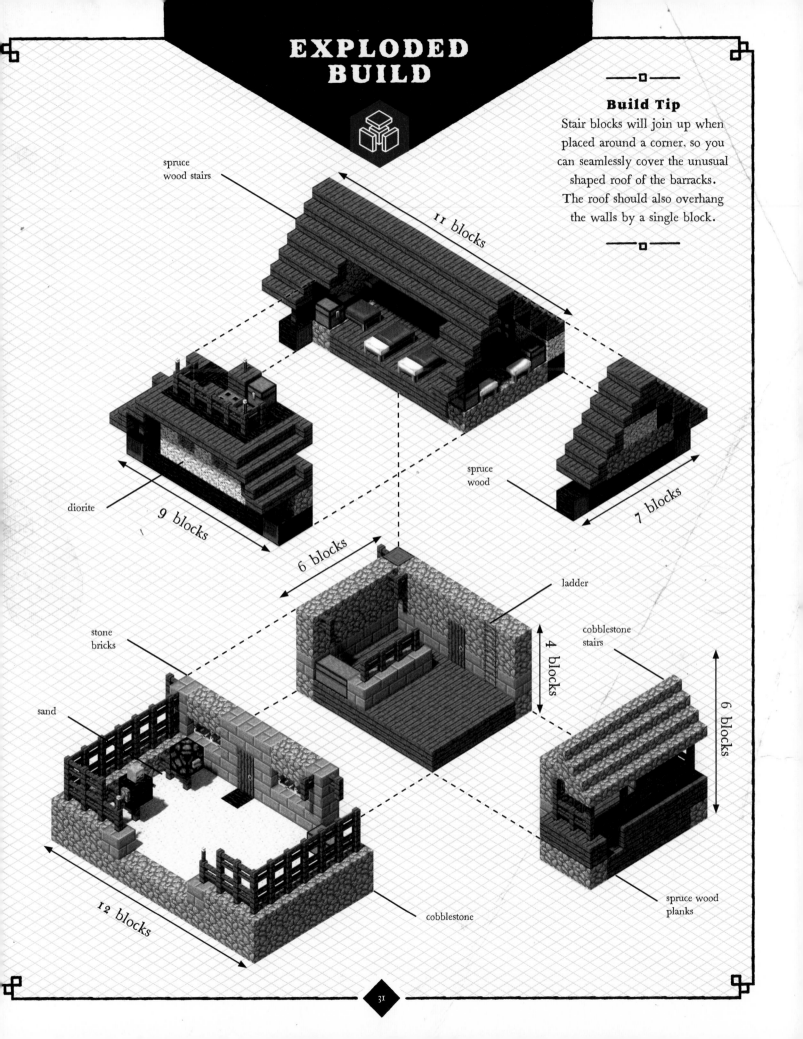

Build Tip

Stair blocks will join up when placed around a corner, so you can seamlessly cover the unusual shaped roof of the barracks. The roof should also overhang the walls by a single block.

spruce wood stairs

11 blocks

diorite

9 blocks

6 blocks

spruce wood

7 blocks

ladder

cobblestone stairs

4 blocks

6 blocks

stone bricks

sand

spruce wood planks

cobblestone

12 blocks

MIX IT UP

Now your troops have somewhere to practise before charging into battle, but the barracks can serve multiple functions for your army - crafting weapons, practising combat and much more. Consider these additions to get your clan fighting fit and ready for war.

◆ Castle Annex

Instead of having the barracks separate from the castle, it can be built as an annex on the side of the keep. If ranks are growing rapidly, a multi-level annex would be the best option to house all the troops, as well as strategy rooms, practice areas and storage holds.

Make a clever target by putting a button on a redstone lamp. If the button is hit with an arrow, the lamp will light up.

Store the best horse armour in nearby chests for when soldiers have to gallop into battle.

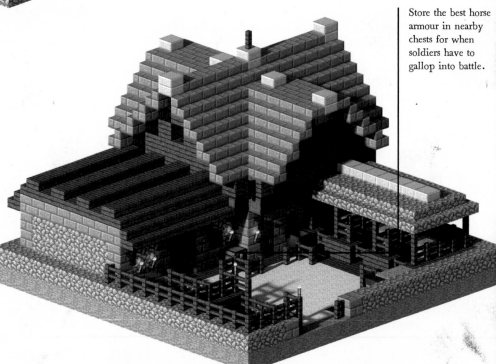

Animal Sheds

Human soldiers don't have to surge into battle alone. Cavalrymen can charge at the enemy on horseback, whilst loyal dogs can also lend a helping paw and attack hostile forces independently. This comfortable annex can store the fastest horses and the most fearsome wolves.

Forge

The kingdom's army needs the best weapons and they need them in working order. A forge within the barracks means that soldiers can create the best weapons and armour, and repair them on anvils if they get broken.

Create a blacksmith's forge with flaming netherrack placed inside a large chimney.

Training Arena

However large an army may be, unless they're well-trained, they'll be useless in a battle. An arena gives soldiers the chance to test their skills against one another, and practise using different offensive tactics.

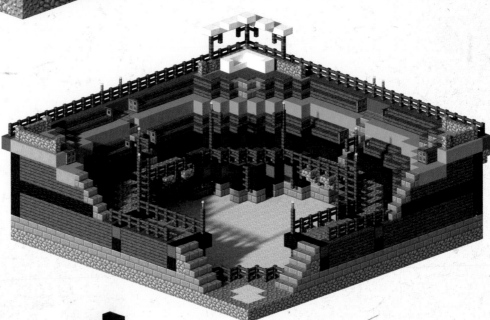

Add a slab to the wall and put a bed on top to make bunks and save space.

Dormitory

As the royal empire grows, so will its army, and they're going to need somewhere to live. Dorms should be created in the barracks, with lots of beds and storage for each brave warrior. The more people that can fit in, the stronger an army will be.

ENCHANTING ROOM

🕐 1 HOUR ❶ ❷ ⬡ ⬡ EASY

If attackers are starting to cause you problems and are on the verge of breaching your stronghold's defences, a bit of magic might be just the thing you need to turn the battle around. Send your best mages and wizards to the enchanting room to cook up potions to buff your clan - or weaken the invaders - and create special arrows that could tip the balance in your favour.

During medieval times lots of people believed in necromancy - using magic to bring back the dead, hence all the myths of zombies and resurrection.

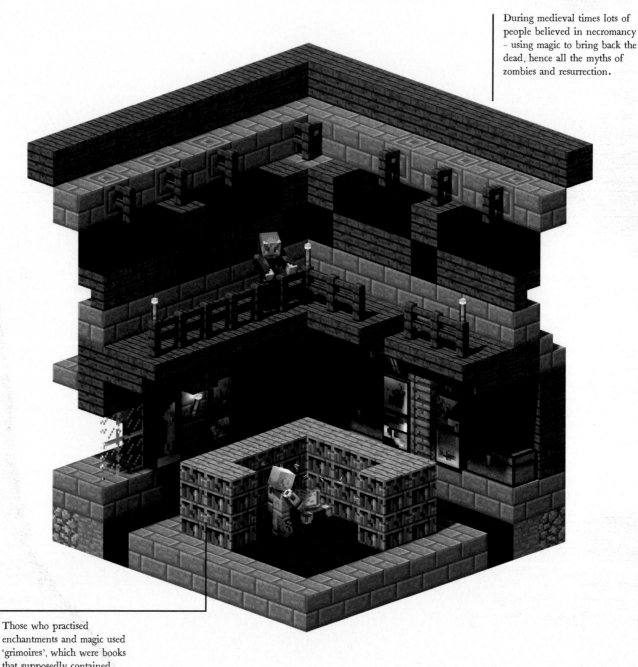

Those who practised enchantments and magic used 'grimoires', which were books that supposedly contained spells and instructions to make magical items.

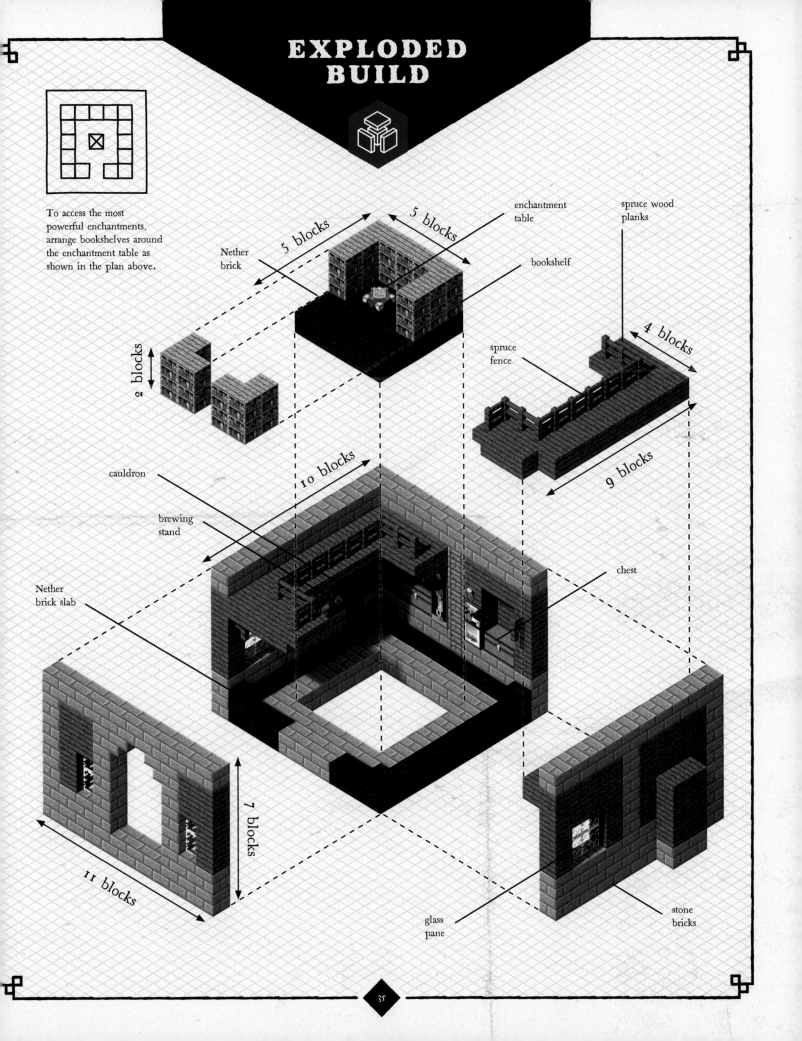

EXPLODED BUILD

To access the most powerful enchantments, arrange bookshelves around the enchantment table as shown in the plan above.

enchantment table

spruce wood planks

5 blocks

5 blocks

5 blocks

Nether brick

bookshelf

2 blocks

spruce fence

4 blocks

9 blocks

cauldron

10 blocks

brewing stand

chest

Nether brick slab

7 blocks

11 blocks

glass pane

stone bricks

MIX IT UP

A magical place like the enchanting room can benefit from a few mystical additions. Whether it's a route to an ethereal dimension, or a well-organised storage system, these extra builds have everything you need to become a master mage.

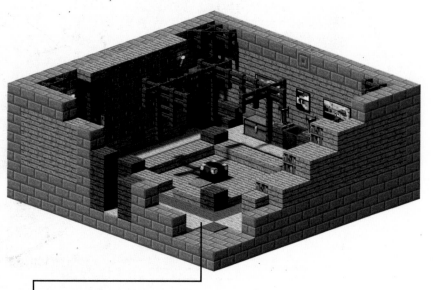

This is how the room will look before stepping on the pressure plate.

ⓘ Hidden Library

Bookshelves correctly arranged around an enchantment table will increase the level of enchanting, but they can create a big obstacle in the middle of the room. This levitating library, operated by a pressure plate, will only appear when someone is standing in front of the table, ready to buff their weapons and armour.

ⓘ How To Make It

The build has three levels – the bottom one has a simple redstone lattice. The middle level is a ring of clay blocks topped with redstone, with sticky pistons on the inside of the ring, facing upwards. The top layer has the ring of bookshelves on top of the sticky pistons, the pressure plate and the enchantment table. The pressure plate and enchantment table both need a wooden block underneath them. When the plate is stepped on, a redstone current surges through the wooden blocks, powering the lattice of redstone and activating the sticky pistons, which in turn push the bookshelves up.

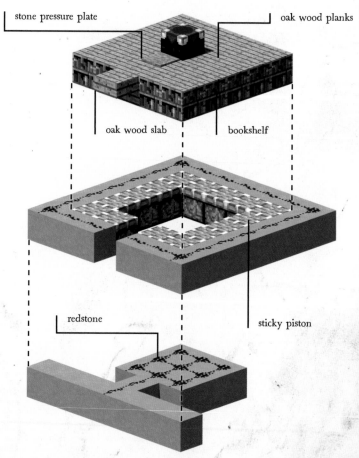

stone pressure plate

oak wood planks

oak wood slab

bookshelf

redstone

sticky piston

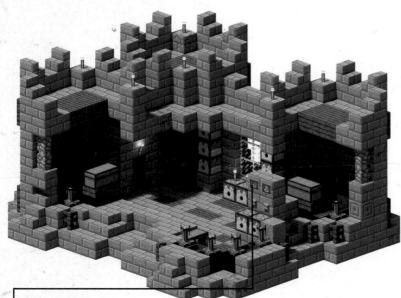

Potion Dispensers

Brewing can take up a lot of inventory space, with the various ingredients required, and the potions that brewing can create. Resources should be invested in a dispensing wall, with a different stash of potions stored in each of the dispensers. Pressing a button will pop them back out when they're needed.

Signs or item frames by each dispenser can be used to label the various potions.

Wizard's Tower

If a wizard needs residence in the castle at all times, the enchanting room can be included within the keep, or attached to the exterior keep walls. This means that there will always be a master magician available to serve the kingdom if trouble starts. The exterior style could be adapted to make it look like a crooked wizard's tower.

Activate the portal with flint and steel, or a fire charge.

The biggest Nether portal that can be made is 23 blocks high by 23 blocks wide.

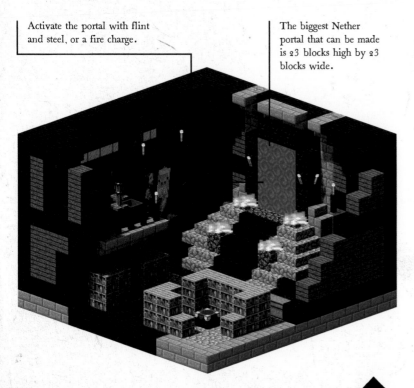

Nether Room

Some of the rarest blocks, often used in brewing and enchanting, can be found in the Nether, so it makes perfect sense to have an easy route there to collect items. Build a 4 x 5-block frame out of obsidian in the enchanting room to create a portal.

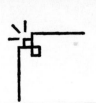

DUNGEON

🕐 **1 HOUR** **1 2** ⬡⬡ **EASY**

When the invasion of your castle has failed and your enemies have surrendered, you'll need to imprison them somewhere to teach them a lesson. A secret, secure dungeon built underneath the castle keep will detain unlucky attackers behind blocks and bars to stop them causing any more trouble.

The dungeons would have been split into individual cells, where as many as ten prisoners would be kept at once.

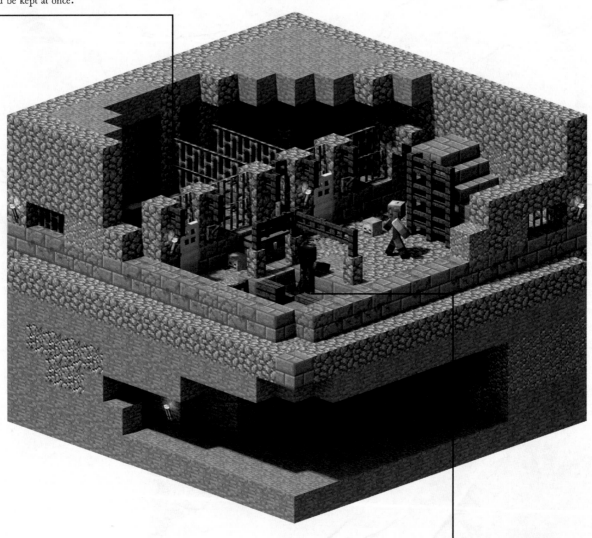

Guardsmen were stationed in dungeons to keep watch over prisoners and ferry them to and from trials.

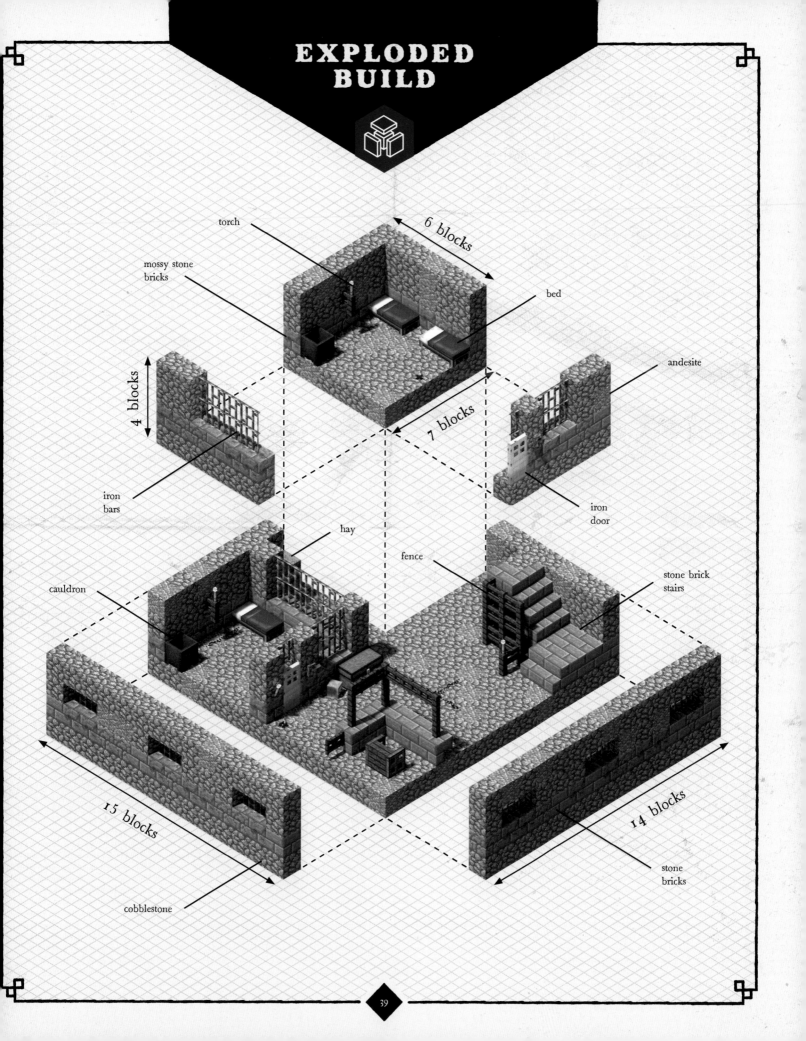

torch

mossy stone bricks

6 blocks

bed

andesite

4 blocks

7 blocks

iron bars

iron door

hay

fence

stone brick stairs

cauldron

stone bricks

15 blocks

14 blocks

cobblestone

MIX IT UP

Are you the kind of ruler who will let their prisoners live in relative comfort, or consign them to wallow in the filthy depths of your dungeon? Use these ideas to ignite your imagination and create an exceptional dungeon that will deter anyone from entering your realm uninvited.

Dungeon Layout

Dungeons can be designed as a single, massive room, or divided into individual cells so each prisoner has their own space. Levers combined with iron doors ensure that they can only be opened by guards on the outside of the cells.

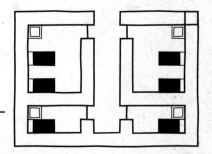

This plan shows a basic layout of cells in a small dungeon, but as many cells as necessary can be added.

Impenetrable Walls

Invading clans may try to launch an assault on the dungeon to free their members. A siege-safe dungeon can be made by filling walls with a curtain of lava to hurt anyone foolish enough to try to break through.

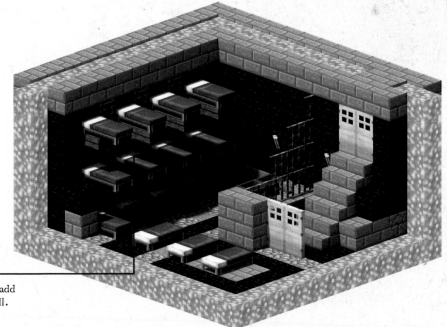

If the dungeon is overflowing with captured enemies, add layers of bunks along the wall to accommodate them all.

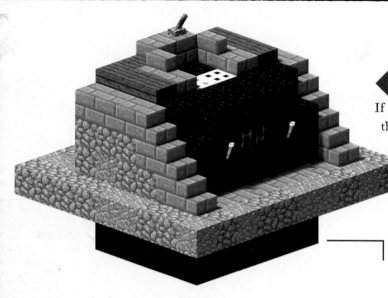

Oubliette

If a prisoner is causing problems with the other inmates, they can be given a lengthy spell in the oubliette – a special type of dungeon accessible only through the ceiling. Create a lever-controlled trapdoor on top of a small obsidian room to drop them down into the lonely pit.

The bottom of the pit should be built below floor level to keep the troublesome prisoner out of sight.

Basic Dungeon

The dungeon doesn't need to be extravagant – it's only going to be used by the raiders and thieves after all. If the kingdom is running low on resources, wood and dirt blocks can be used to make a dungeon, then replaced with stronger blocks when possible.

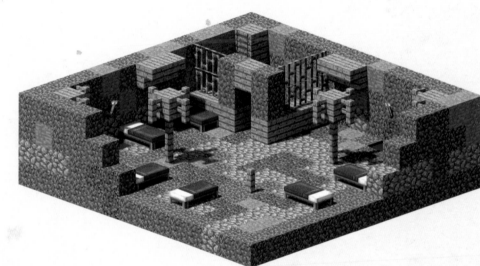

Prisoners can dig through dirt without tools, so build a basic dungeon deep enough so they can't find their way back to the surface.

iron maiden

stretch rack

Torture Chamber

This dark, dank room is reserved for the worst mobs that stumble upon the kingdom. Filled with gloriously creative inventions and devices of discomfort, some rulers may deem this room too cruel even for creepers and zombies.

dunking stool

VILLAGE

VILLAGE HOUSE

🕐 **1 HOUR** **1** ② ③ ④ **BEGINNER**

A medieval kingdom needs loyal subjects to rule over and they need somewhere to live too.
Build lots of these basic houses to create somewhere for your villagers to live, thrive and
hide from hostile mobs at night. Use simple blocks like wood and cobblestone to
recreate the simple style of buildings that were around in medieval times.

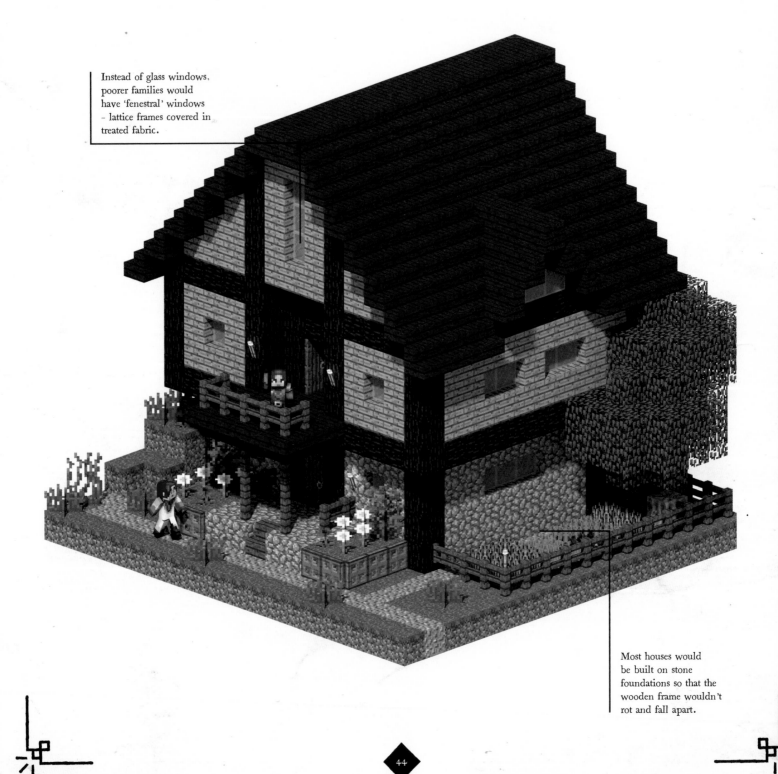

Instead of glass windows,
poorer families would
have 'fenestral' windows
– lattice frames covered in
treated fabric.

Most houses would
be built on stone
foundations so that the
wooden frame wouldn't
rot and fall apart.

EXPLODED BUILD

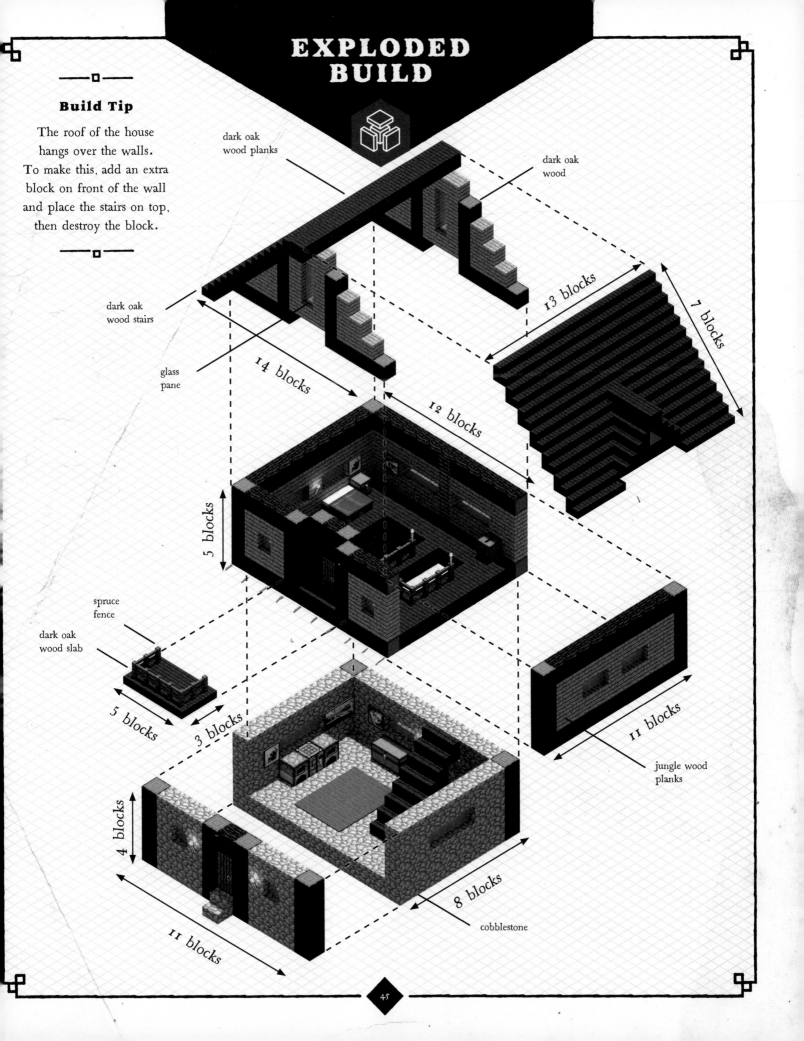

Build Tip

The roof of the house hangs over the walls. To make this, add an extra block on front of the wall and place the stairs on top, then destroy the block.

dark oak wood planks

dark oak wood

dark oak wood stairs

glass pane

13 blocks

7 blocks

14 blocks

12 blocks

5 blocks

spruce fence

dark oak wood slab

5 blocks

3 blocks

11 blocks

jungle wood planks

4 blocks

8 blocks

cobblestone

11 blocks

45

MIX IT UP

A village full of identical houses would look boring, but there are lots of things you can do to make each dwelling unique. Of course you can change the shape of the buildings and the blocks they are constructed from, but there are lots of different features you can add too.

Medieval Bungalow

To create a difference between the houses of the village, some of them can be built with just a ground floor. Adding walls inside the house would make the rooms really small, so place beds, furnaces and other household furniture in the same space, without any partitions.

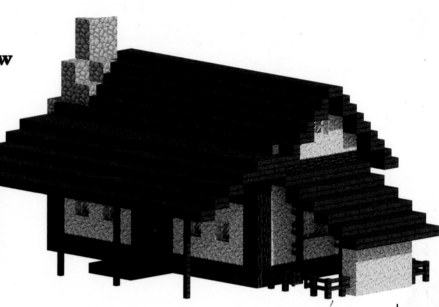

Wooden trapdoors can be used for a simple open-window effect.

An annex on the side of a house, with a roof and space to roam, is perfect for keeping pets.

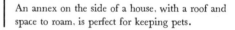 Elevated House

Build a house on top of a sturdy ground floor so that villagers can live safely out of the reach of spiders, creepers and other hostile mobs. The lower floor is only accessible from the interior of the house, so it's the perfect place to install a panic room, or tunnel leading to a secret exit, just in case the village is attacked.

The bottom floor of the house can be used as a storage room.

Add support pillars to the staircase using cobblestone fence blocks.

Add cobwebs to the top of a chimney to
make it look like it's spouting smoke.

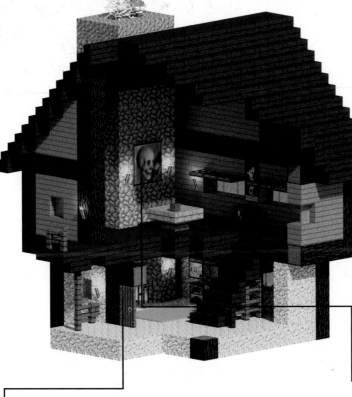

Interior Decoration

Adding exciting decorations to houses can make them much
more attractive places to live. Different combinations
of plants, flowers, torches, crafting tables, furnaces,
signs, paintings and customisable item frames will
create unique houses. Avoid anything too modern
though, like the jukebox.

Fortress Facts

Pets kept in medieval
times always served a
purpose. Dogs were
used for security
and hunting, whilst
cats would catch rats
around the house.

Paintings can cover a space on
a wall of up to 4 x 4 blocks.
To make a painting appear
at this size, the painting will
need to be placed on the
bottom-left square of the space.

Make a fireplace by placing netherrack blocks
in the floor, then light it with flint and steel.

Rural House

Further out from the castle walls, in bigger sections
of land, there should be more rural houses, with
huge, open expanses around them. The land can
be used to plant carrots, wheat, pumpkins and
more so that villagers can trade with others
at the market.

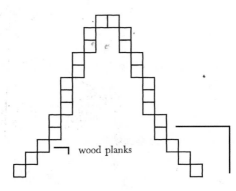

wood planks

The roof can be made tall
and curvy by stacking wood
blocks on top of each other at
certain points.

Surround crops with a fence to
stop any wild animals ruining them.

MARKET SQUARE

⏱ **1 HOUR**   **1** ② ③ ④   **BEGINNER**

The market square is the hub of commerce and activity in your medieval kingdom. Everything you could possibly need for your kingdom can be found at one of the stalls in the square. Townspeople will be trading everything from weapons and potions to crops like pumpkins and potatoes.

Traders would have specialised in selling a single type of item. Grocers would sell food, blacksmiths offered weapons and metalwork, whilst farmers would trade in livestock.

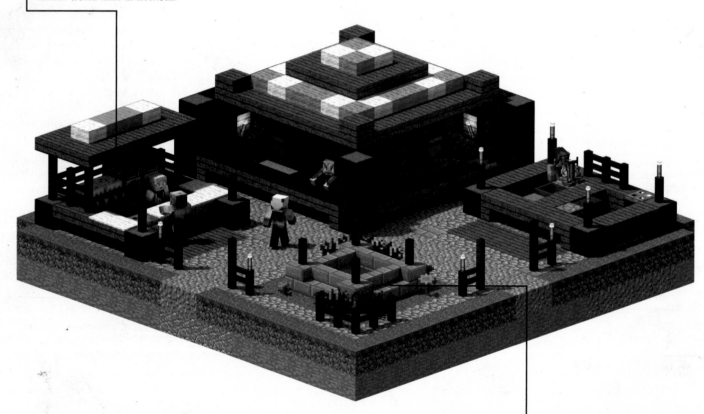

Markets were the heart of any town. In fact, the very definition of a town, as opposed to a village, used to be that it had a market.

EXPLODED BUILD

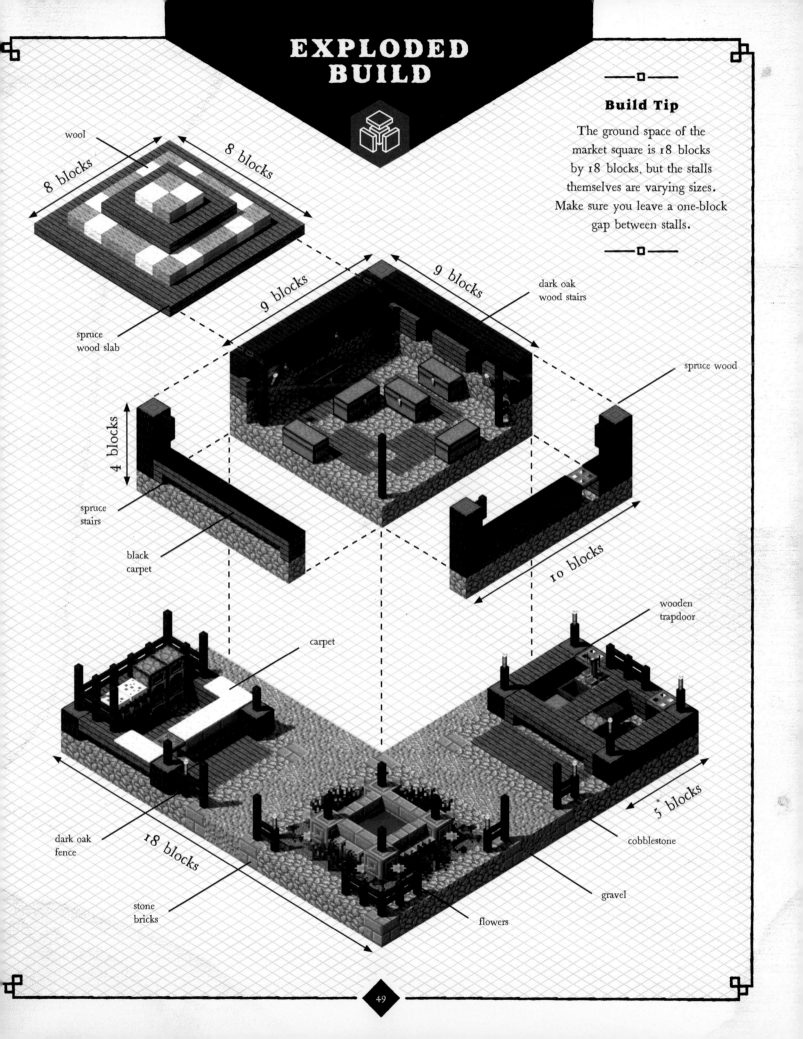

Build Tip

The ground space of the market square is 18 blocks by 18 blocks, but the stalls themselves are varying sizes. Make sure you leave a one-block gap between stalls.

wool

8 blocks

8 blocks

spruce wood slab

9 blocks

9 blocks

dark oak wood stairs

spruce wood

4 blocks

spruce stairs

black carpet

10 blocks

carpet

wooden trapdoor

dark oak fence

18 blocks

stone bricks

flowers

cobblestone

gravel

5 blocks

MIX IT UP

Just like NPC villagers, the market square will offer the opportunity to make some clever trades. With a few additions and a bit of customisation, you'll have people flocking from all over to admire the features of your market and join in the hustle and bustle of your trading district.

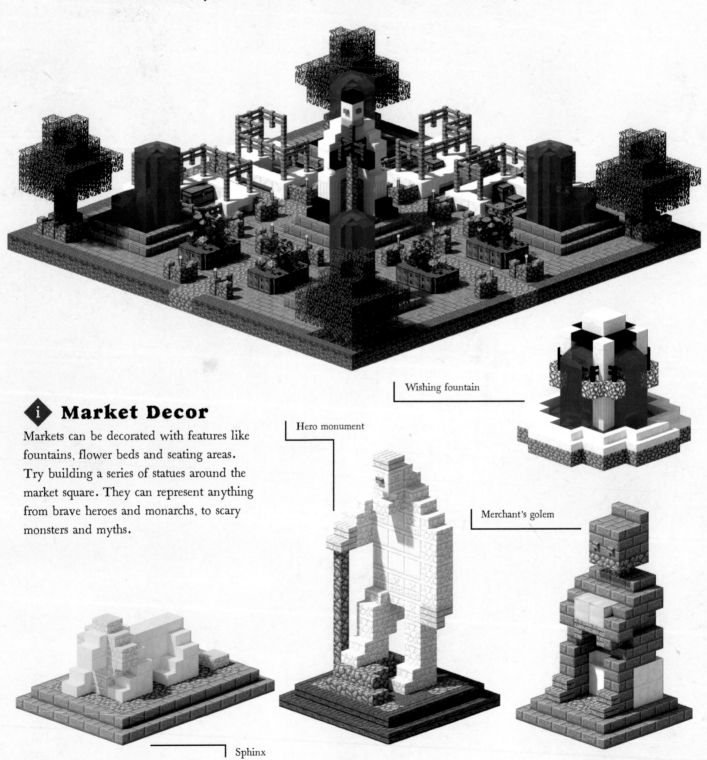

Wishing fountain

Hero monument

Merchant's golem

ℹ Market Decor

Markets can be decorated with features like fountains, flower beds and seating areas. Try building a series of statues around the market square. They can represent anything from brave heroes and monarchs, to scary monsters and myths.

Sphinx

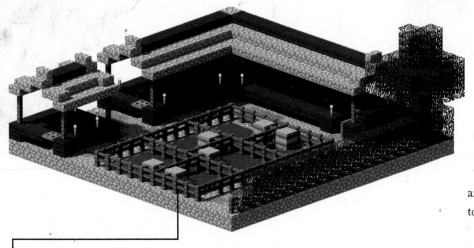

Livestock Trading

If villagers find themselves with an abundance of animals, they can take these to market too. Pigs, sheep, chickens and other useful animals can all be traded. These could be used to provide eggs, meat and milk to the buyer, or as a source of items to trade at future markets.

Each trader would have their own enclosure for their animals. Create each one using simple fenced areas and hay bales.

Trade Quarter

Some traders may want to set up shop within buildings rather than on stalls, either because they have outgrown a small stall, or because they deal in more valuable items like rare ores, and need a more secure place to trade from. These shops provide the perfect surrounding to the market square and keep everything in one place.

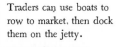

Traders can use boats to row to market, then dock them on the jetty.

Dockside Market

Fishing is another easy way to gain items to trade. Fish caught at sea can be used to replenish health and hunger, while the rest can be traded so someone else can benefit from the fishy haul. Build stalls around a jetty on the water and add a dock-master's house as well.

TRAVELLERS' TAVERN

🕐 1.5 HOURS ❶ ❷ ③ ④ EASY

Lots of people will want to visit your medieval fortress, but not all of them will be able to fit in the castle.
However, if you build a tavern, then friends, travellers and merchants will have a place to stay, socialise
with the townsfolk and replenish their energy with bowls of rabbit stew or beetroot soup.

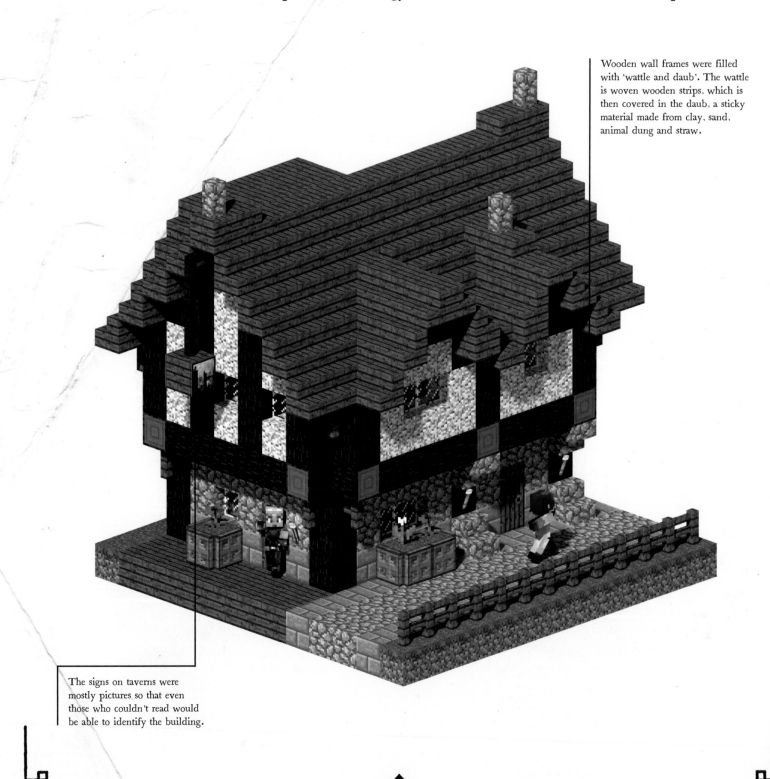

Wooden wall frames were filled
with 'wattle and daub'. The wattle
is woven wooden strips, which is
then covered in the daub, a sticky
material made from clay, sand,
animal dung and straw.

The signs on taverns were
mostly pictures so that even
those who couldn't read would
be able to identify the building.

EXPLODED BUILD

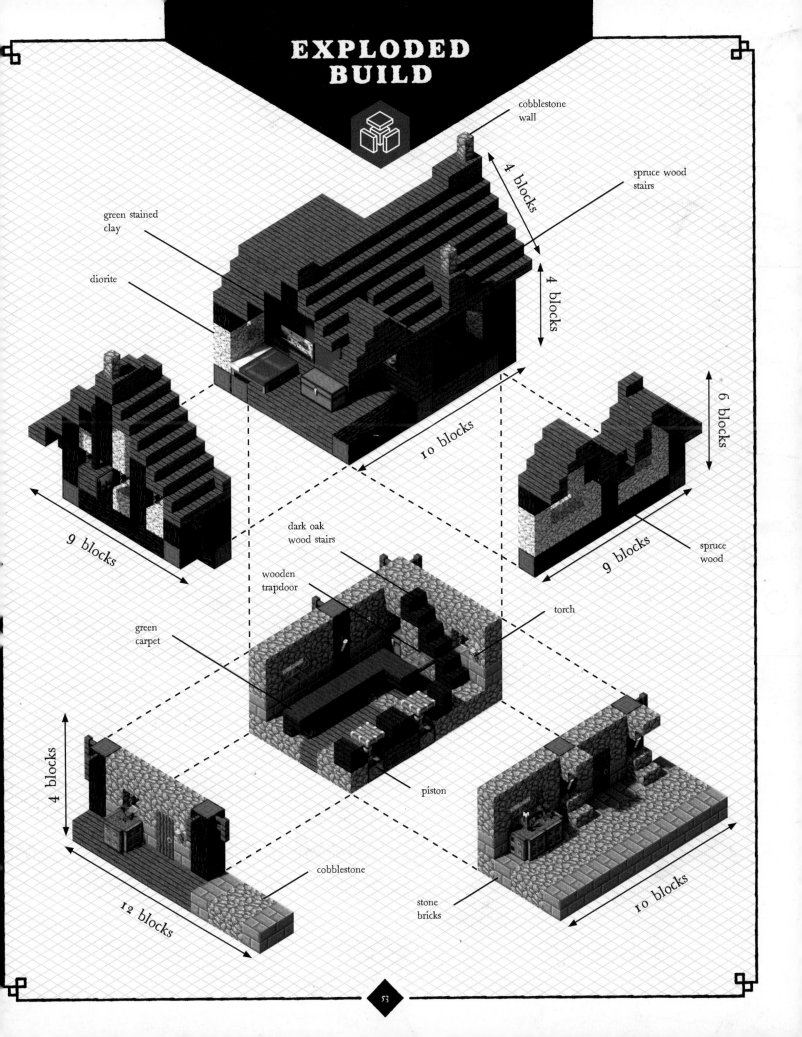

cobblestone wall

spruce wood stairs

4 blocks

4 blocks

green stained clay

diorite

6 blocks

10 blocks

9 blocks

9 blocks

spruce wood

dark oak wood stairs

wooden trapdoor

torch

green carpet

piston

4 blocks

cobblestone

stone bricks

12 blocks

10 blocks

MIX IT UP

Taverns are the social heart of villages, and they can take many shapes and forms depending on where they are, or what the villagers need. Add some of these builds and variations to your tavern to provide comforts to visitors and locals alike.

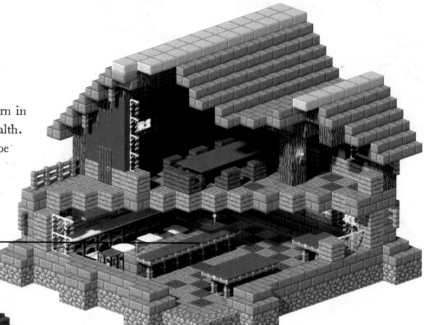

Tavern Eatery

Weary travellers will arrive at the village tavern in need of food to replenish their hunger and health. Placing lots of furnaces means that meals can be made for many customers at once, as long as the pantry is well-stocked with ingredients.

Place carpet on top of piston tables to make tablecloths.

A boarding house can contain more than bedrooms - add private seating rooms, dining areas and a greeting hall on the ground floor.

Boarding House

The busiest taverns will be situated in the biggest towns, and could welcome dozens of visitors at any one time. Multiple floors will be necessary to provide enough room for every traveller, merchant and mercenary who passes through the kingdom.

The bedrooms in a boarding house should only contain necessities like a bed and storage space.

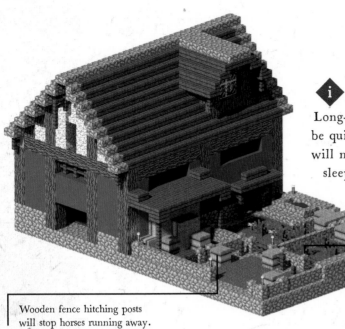

Stables

Long-distance travel through the vast kingdom will be quicker and easier on horseback, so travellers will need somewhere for their trusty steeds to sleep overnight. A large barn outside the tavern, complete with comfy hay bales and plenty of carrots should be enough to house tired horses.

Wooden fence hitching posts will stop horses running away.

Make sure there is plenty of outdoor space for the horses to roam around.

Taverns can be made more inviting by adding potted plants - use dirt blocks, trapdoors and flowers.

Fortress Facts

Inns and taverns would have been particularly important outside of major towns. They would be one of the only places along a road in which travellers could find food and a place to sleep.

A tavern complex can be made with any number of buildings, connected by a series of elevated passages.

Taverns in Towns

Building big taverns in busy, populated towns is difficult, but can be done by combining buildings. An elevated walkway connecting buildings will allow horses, carts and villagers to use the roads and path below, and offer an extended space for bedrooms in the taverns.

CATHEDRAL

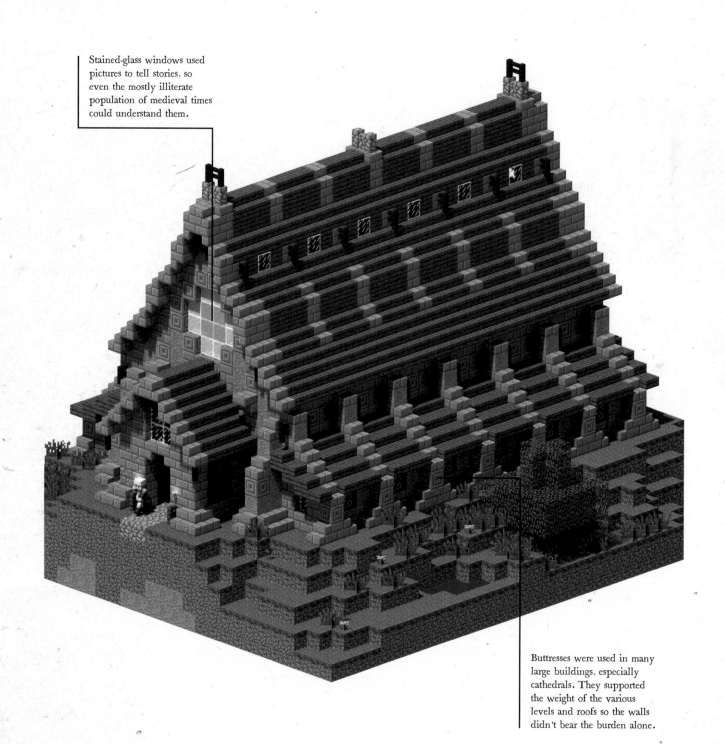

🕐 2 HOURS ❶❷❸④ INTERMEDIATE

The biggest and most elaborate building in your kingdom, besides your castle, will be the cathedral. With colourful stained glass, combinations of different block shapes and the capacity to hold hundreds, even thousands, of townspeople, it will be one of the busiest places in your entire fortress.

Stained-glass windows used pictures to tell stories, so even the mostly illiterate population of medieval times could understand them.

Buttresses were used in many large buildings, especially cathedrals. They supported the weight of the various levels and roofs so the walls didn't bear the burden alone.

EXPLODED BUILD

Build Tip

With a big complicated build like the cathedral, start by creating the main layout of the floor, before building up to make the walls and roof.

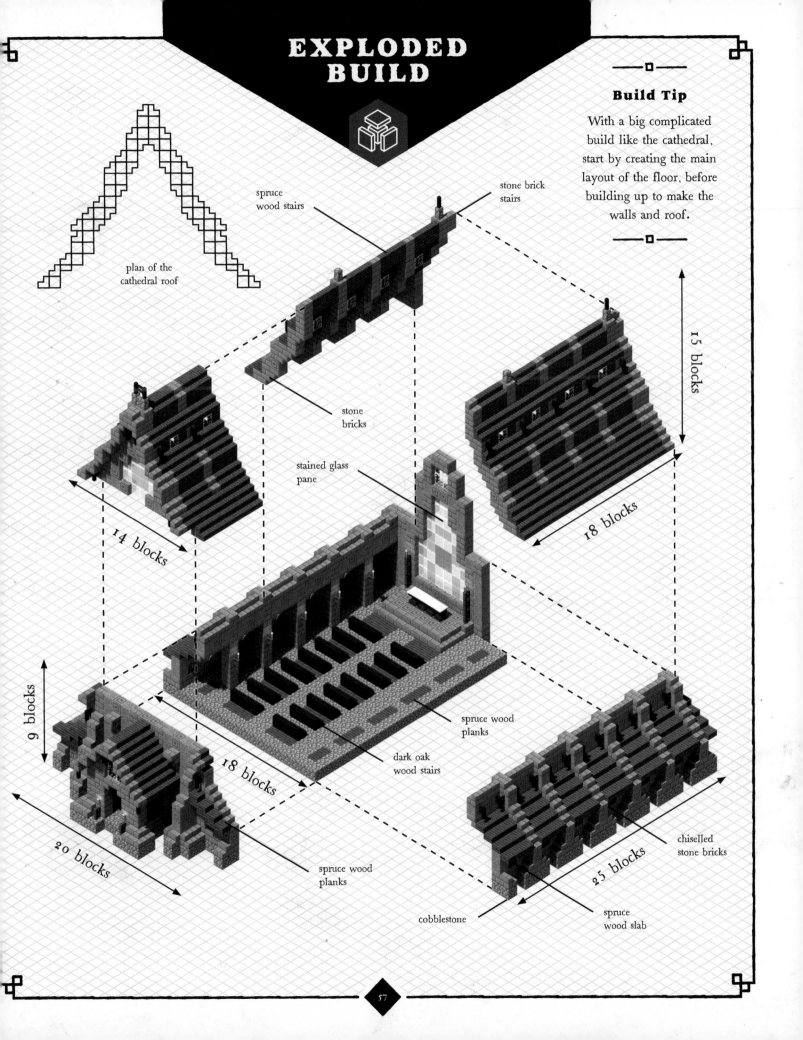

plan of the cathedral roof

spruce wood stairs

stone brick stairs

stone bricks

stained glass pane

15 blocks

18 blocks

14 blocks

spruce wood planks

dark oak wood stairs

9 blocks

18 blocks

chiselled stone bricks

20 blocks

25 blocks

spruce wood planks

cobblestone

spruce wood slab

MIX IT UP

You've just made the centre of your village community, the cathedral, where the masses will gather for all sorts of events. Try out some of these additions and variations to properly represent your growing congregation.

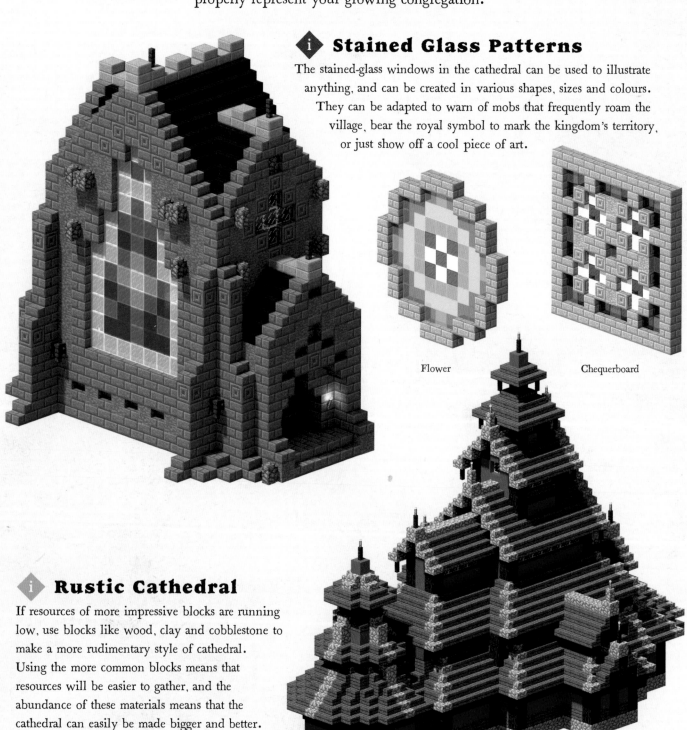

ⓘ Stained Glass Patterns

The stained-glass windows in the cathedral can be used to illustrate anything, and can be created in various shapes, sizes and colours. They can be adapted to warn of mobs that frequently roam the village, bear the royal symbol to mark the kingdom's territory, or just show off a cool piece of art.

Flower   Chequerboard

ⓘ Rustic Cathedral

If resources of more impressive blocks are running low, use blocks like wood, clay and cobblestone to make a more rudimentary style of cathedral. Using the more common blocks means that resources will be easier to gather, and the abundance of these materials means that the cathedral can easily be made bigger and better.

Bell Tower

Cathedrals should have a bell tower, or belfry, which can be used to call people to the cathedral, announce the time of day, or to sound an alarm to the villagers. Build a tall bell tower into the cathedral so that people can hear it for miles around.

> Decorative crenellations, like those also featured on castles, can be added to cathedrals too.

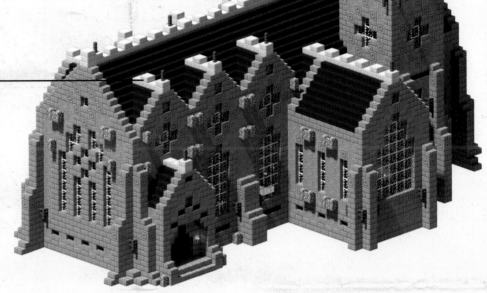

 ## Note Block Bell

A working bell system can be created inside the tower using note blocks. The sound that a note block makes will differ depending on the type of block that it's placed on. Dirt blocks will make a piano sound, which is the closest to a bell sound you can get. The pitch of a note block can be altered by interacting with it too.

Note Block Bell System

The circuit for the cathedral bell is straightforward enough and doesn't require a massive amount of resources. The example to the right has three pairs of note blocks, with repeaters set to sound them at different times. It's possible to have dozens of different note blocks, but it could get a bit noisy.

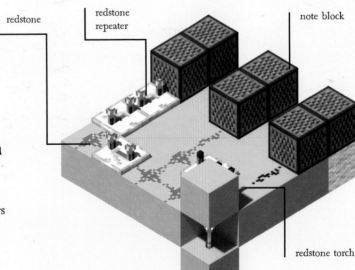

redstone

redstone repeater

note block

redstone torch

FINISHING TOUCHES

Now you have a complete village for your subjects to live, trade and socialise in, it's time to add a few extra features to make it feel like home. From the decorative to the functional, these simple builds will give your village a distinct medieval feel.

Beacons

Create fiery columns using netherrack to serve as medieval beacons, used to signal other villages or outposts. They can be modified to serve as lamp posts to illuminate the streets at night, or built into a lighthouse at the docks so seafarers can find land.

Use contrasting coloured blocks to help beacons stand out in the distance.

Flags

Flags are used to mark the kingdom's territory, so fly them over the village and castle to show which empire they belong to. They can be created with coloured wool and wood blocks.

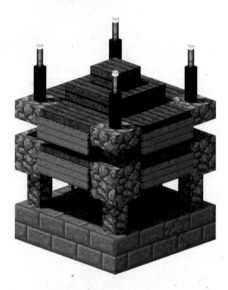

Noticeboard

Villagers can keep up to date with all the events and news in the kingdom by visiting the notice board, created with wooden stairs, cobblestone blocks and slabs. Anyone can add a sign if they want to make an announcement to the public, making it a valuable resource for the community.

Use leads to hitch horses to the fences on the front of carts.

Carts

Build wooden carts to decorate the rural parts of the village. Create them using trapdoors, signs, fences and hay bales. They can be used to tether wandering animals or stash crops.

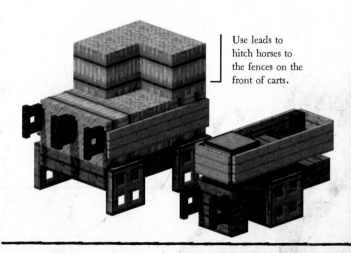

Storage Hold

Villagers can use storage holds to share tools and resources for the town. They could include things like axes to chop down trees, ores to be used for crafting, or even weapons to help the villagers fend off attacks before the royal army arrives to help.

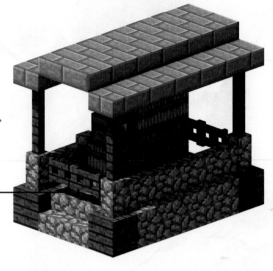

Gates will stop stray mobs from entering the hold and becoming trapped.

Signage

Kingdoms are huge places, so villagers need to be able to find their way around easily. Signposts along pathways and intersections can point the way to the major landmarks in the village and beyond.

Item frames can be used instead of signs - for instance, a sword in an item frame would show the way to the barracks.

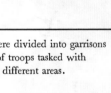

Guard Post

Villages aren't as well fortified as castles, but loyal subjects still need to be protected. Soldiers stationed at guard posts around the village perimeter will be enough to spot impending threats and keep them safe from harm.

Armies were divided into garrisons - groups of troops tasked with protecting different areas.

Well

Water is a necessity in any village, so water sources such as wells were very important. People can fill up buckets of water to douse fires, irrigate their crops and fill their cauldrons, all without leaving the safety of their kingdom. Place water source blocks in a cobblestone pool to make your well.

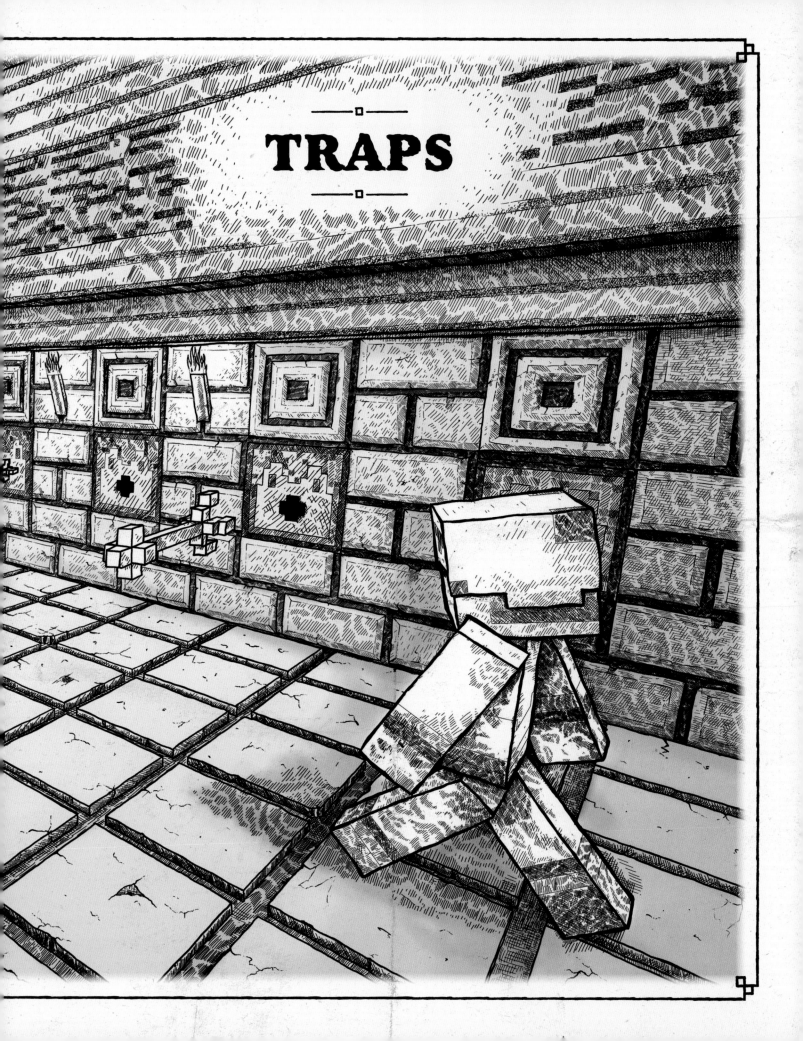

LAVA TRAP ROOM

⏱ **2 HOURS** ❶❷③④ **EASY**

Castles had plenty of traps to thwart invaders getting their hands on the royal riches, but most of them were on the outside. However, in Minecraft you can build traps directly into your keep. This lava trap room will draw in enemies with the promise of a chest full of loot, then release a huge pool of lava, without any way of escaping. You can build this room into any part of your castle.

Similar to the lava trap room, there were many weapons and defences that utilised fire, boiling liquids or heat during medieval times. These were known as 'thermal weapons'.

'Greek fire' was a thermal weapon used at sea to keep invaders away from land. A flammable solution would be poured into the sea and lit, creating a fire on top of the water, burning any boats that it touched.

EXPLODED BUILD

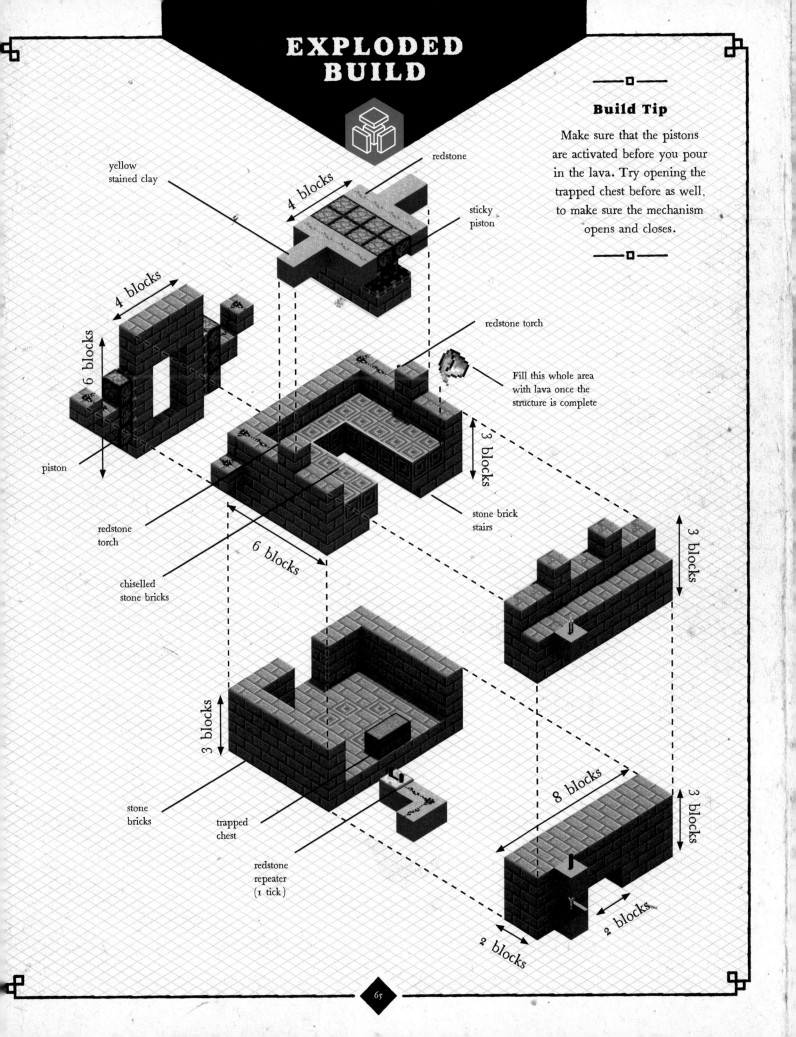

Build Tip

Make sure that the pistons are activated before you pour in the lava. Try opening the trapped chest before as well, to make sure the mechanism opens and closes.

redstone

yellow stained clay

sticky piston

4 blocks

4 blocks

6 blocks

redstone torch

Fill this whole area with lava once the structure is complete

piston

3 blocks

redstone torch

stone brick stairs

chiselled stone bricks

6 blocks

3 blocks

3 blocks

stone bricks

trapped chest

3 blocks

redstone repeater (1 tick)

8 blocks

2 blocks

2 blocks

2 blocks

GETTING IT RIGHT

The lava trap room relies on a redstone circuit to trigger the release of lava and the shutting of the door. The trap uses parallel redstone circuits to trigger both mechanisms at the same time, using a sneaky trapped chest to lure in greedy invaders. Follow this guide to make your first trap.

1 Redstone Arrangement

The redstone circuit is split into two sections. The first section controls the release of the lava, whilst the second covers the exit. The first section is separated from the second by a single brick block, with a redstone torch on the side. Once the redstone circuit is complete, the first part will be powered, but the second part won't receive any power due to the intervening block.

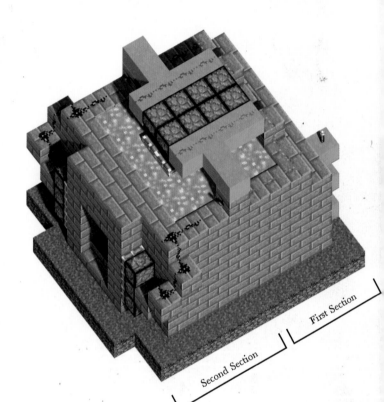

First Section

Second Section

Avoid using any flammable blocks near the lava, such as wood or wool.

2 Vertical Circuit

When the trapped chest is opened, it sends a small redstone charge to a redstone repeater, which amplifies the charge and sends it along the circuit. When it reaches the block that the first redstone torch is on, the circuit moves up vertically using alternating redstone torches. This can be used to make any circuit travel upwards, as long as there are an odd number of torches in the arrangement.

Make sure the arrow on the repeater is facing towards the redstone on the next block.

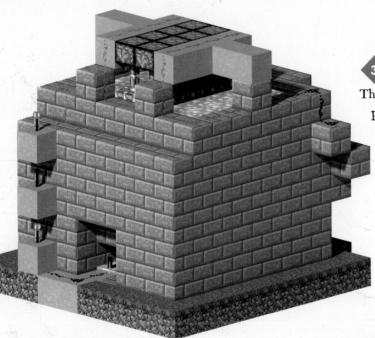

3 Lava Release

The first part of the circuit powers a series of sticky pistons, which hold the lava in a pool supported by stone brick blocks. When the trap is triggered, the power in the first part of the circuit switches off, deactivating the sticky pistons and letting the lava flow.

4 Front Section

The second part of the circuit continues along the top of the room and cascades down to a brick block beside the middle piston. This powers the two pistons adjacent to the middle one. As the first section loses power, the redstone torch on the intervening stone brick block turns on, powering the second part of the circuit.

The redstone torches in the middle of the circuit should be facing the door at the front.

If the circuit is set up correctly, the doors will shut like this.

5 Door Mechanism

When the second part of the circuit is powered, it causes the pistons to push the stone brick blocks over the entrance. The bricks will stay in place, even after the trapped chest is shut, so there's no way for anyone to get out. The lava will clear up after a while, but it will be around long enough to deplete almost all of the enemy's health.

HIDDEN PITFALL

It can be hard to defend a castle under siege, especially if there are only a few friends in your clan. If you can't cover every entrance and exit, you can add this trap instead. Using a series of sticky pistons and a simple tripwire mechanism to reveal a deep pit, you can capture or kill any invader, animal or angry skeleton that dares to trespass in your fortress.

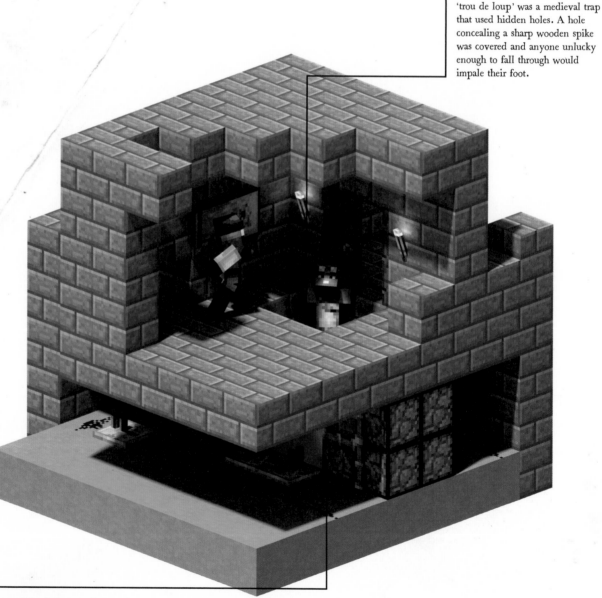

Similar to this Hidden Pitfall, the 'trou de loup' was a medieval trap that used hidden holes. A hole concealing a sharp wooden spike was covered and anyone unlucky enough to fall through would impale their foot.

Pistons have had a practical use in weaponry since the 10th century. In China they used a device called the 'Pen Huo Qi', which was a type of flamethrower powered by two pistons.

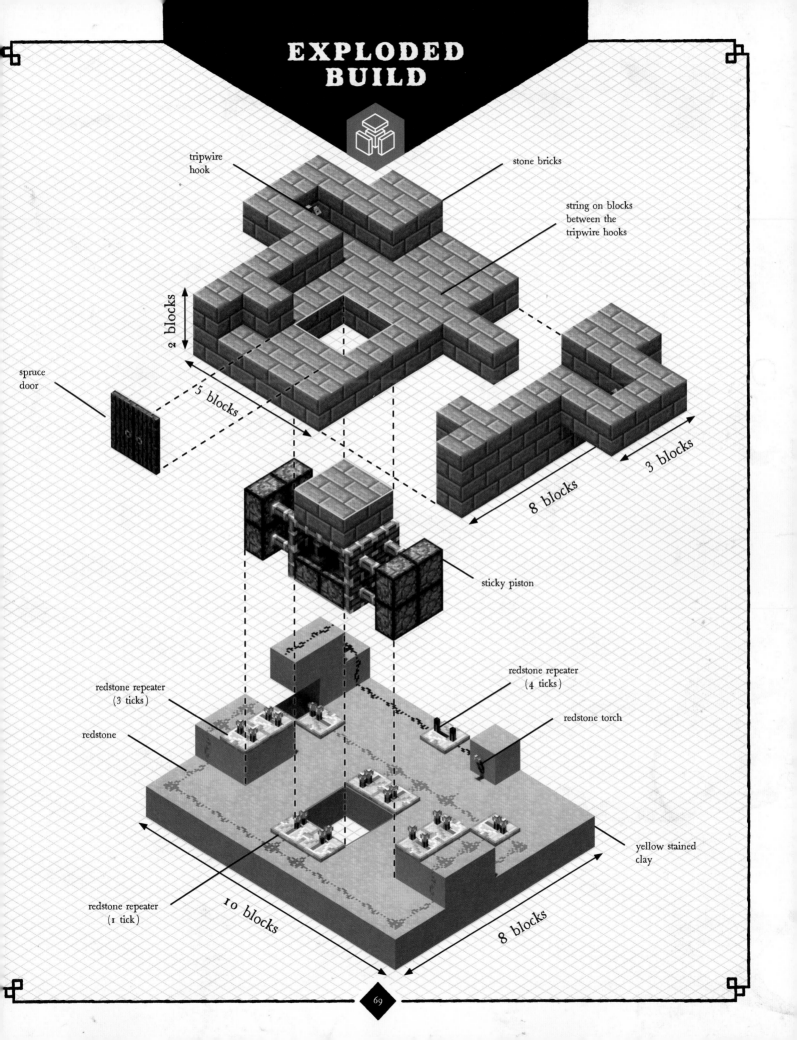

EXPLODED BUILD

tripwire hook

stone bricks

string on blocks between the tripwire hooks

2 blocks

spruce door

5 blocks

3 blocks

8 blocks

sticky piston

redstone repeater (3 ticks)

redstone repeater (4 ticks)

redstone torch

redstone

yellow stained clay

redstone repeater (1 tick)

10 blocks

8 blocks

GETTING IT RIGHT

If created properly, the hidden pitfall is a deadly trap, but it relies on an intricate system to trigger different mechanisms at different times, including repeater delays and piston sequences. Follow these guidelines and your trap will be ready to send intruders plummeting to the bedrock layer.

The string will follow this line.

1 Tripwire Mechanism

The tripwire mechanism consists of two tripwire hooks and string to connect them. In this trap, the hooks are hidden in recesses in the hallway, while the string itself is barely visible. When the tripwire is triggered, the current flows through the back part of the mechanism, turning off the redstone torch and deactivating the front part of the circuit. The tripwire will remain intact, so that the next intruder will set off the same trap.

Make sure there's a block gap between the block the tripwire hook is attached to and the clay blocks underneath, so there is space for the redstone to be placed.

The redstone torch should face the front section of the circuit.

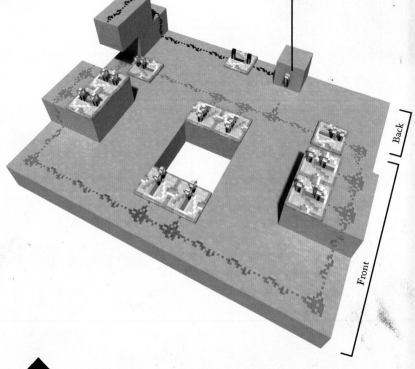

Back

Front

2 Redstone Arrangement

The redstone circuit is split into two parts. The front part controls the pistons, and is powered by a redstone torch. The back part links to the tripwire mechanism above. The two sections are separated by the block that bears the redstone torch. The redstone torch acts as a mediator between the two sections, meaning that they are never activated at the same time.

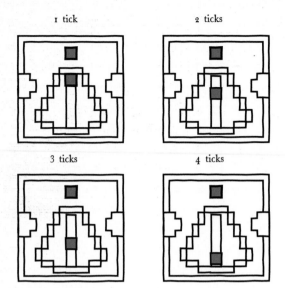

1 tick 2 ticks

3 ticks 4 ticks

3 Repeaters and Ticks

Redstone repeaters can be modified to delay the redstone signal in a circuit. When first placed, repeaters have a delay of 1 redstone 'tick'. It's possible to interact with them and amend the delay to up to 4 redstone ticks. In this circuit, the repeaters delay the current to various mechanisms so that they are deactivated at different times, enabling a more intricate system of pistons.

4 Sequenced Pistons

When an intruder sets the trap off, it stops the current to the pistons in the front part of the trap, and they retract. The repeater delays in the circuit cause the vertical pistons to drop first, bringing them and the four stone brick floor blocks in line with the horizontal pistons. Once they've been pulled down, the horizontal pistons deactivate, pulling the vertical pistons and floor blocks to one side, opening up the massive drop below. When the mechanism activates again, the process reverses, replacing the stone brick floor blocks.

1.

2.

3.

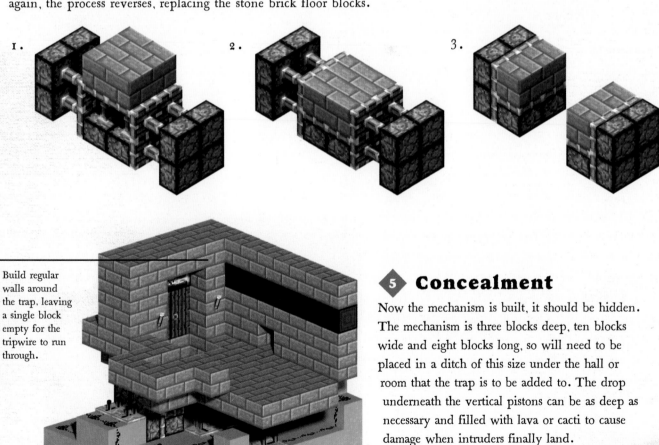

Build regular walls around the trap, leaving a single block empty for the tripwire to run through.

5 Concealment

Now the mechanism is built, it should be hidden. The mechanism is three blocks deep, ten blocks wide and eight blocks long, so will need to be placed in a ditch of this size under the hall or room that the trap is to be added to. The drop underneath the vertical pistons can be as deep as necessary and filled with lava or cacti to cause damage when intruders finally land.

ARROW GAUNTLET

⏱ **2 HOURS** **❶❷❸❹** **INTERMEDIATE**

If invaders make it past all your other defences and are closing in on your position, then this sneaky trap may just save you. You can build it into any wall within your castle, so each and every hallway can be rigged to release a hail of arrows on invaders, or anything else that happens to wander in.

Medieval castles had small passageways called 'murder holes'. When enemies were in these passages, the entrances were blocked, while arrows, hot sand and boiling water were fired at enemies.

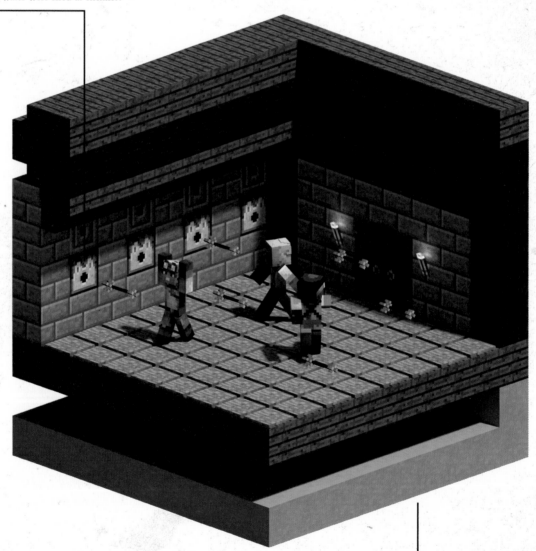

Murder holes were most often found in the gatehouses, where invaders would pass once the exterior gates had been destroyed.

EXPLODED BUILD

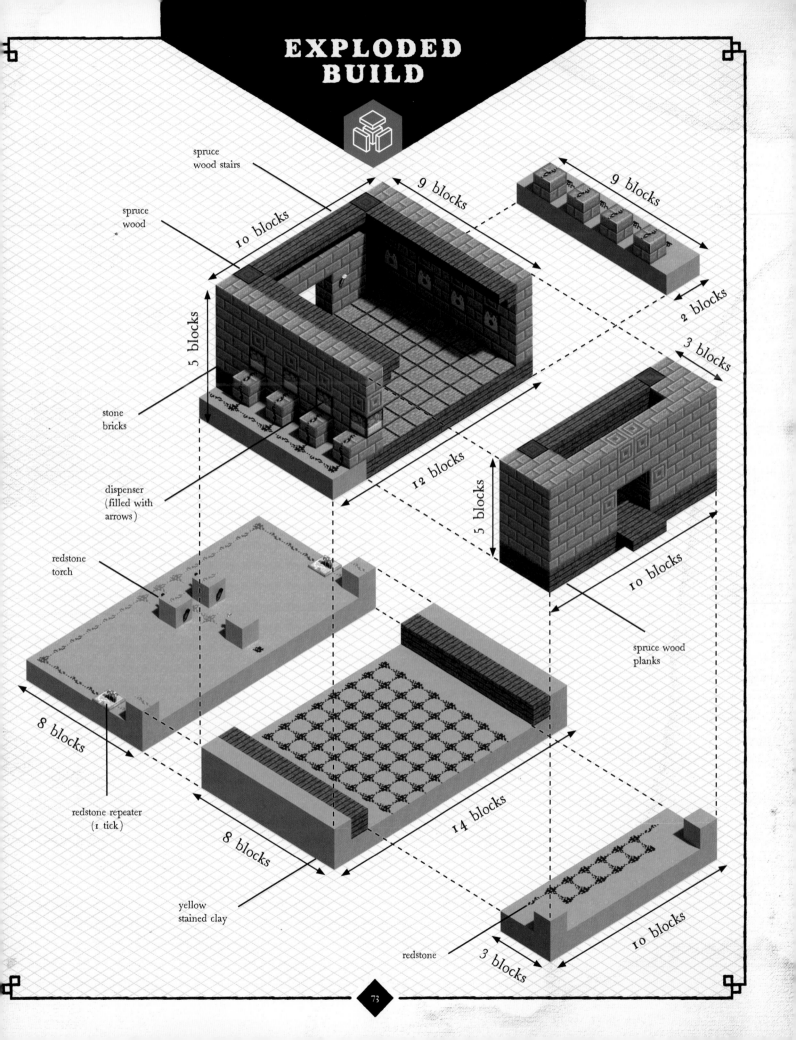

spruce
wood stairs

spruce
wood

10 blocks

9 blocks

9 blocks

2 blocks

5 blocks

stone
bricks

3 blocks

5 blocks

12 blocks

dispenser
(filled with
arrows)

10 blocks

spruce wood
planks

redstone
torch

8 blocks

redstone repeater
(1 tick)

8 blocks

14 blocks

yellow
stained clay

redstone

3 blocks

10 blocks

GETTING IT RIGHT

The arrow gauntlet is one of the simplest traps you can add to your castle, with a very simple redstone circuit triggered by a large set of pressure plates. However, it can also be one of the most dangerous as it covers such a large area, which makes it very difficult to escape alive.

1 Redstone Arrangement

The redstone used in this trap is split into two sections: the lower and upper. The upper section controls the dispensers, while the lower section consists of a grid of redstone. The grid is powered by the stone pressure plates above and a pulse circuit, a simple system that creates a redstone signal that repeatedly reacts to the pressure plates, firing a constant stream of arrows.

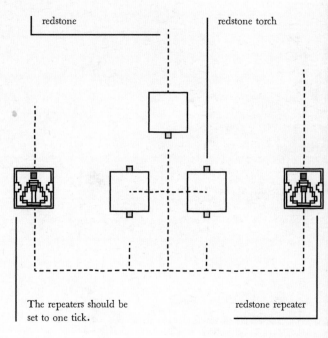

redstone   redstone torch

The repeaters should be set to one tick.

redstone repeater

The wooden floor blocks can be swapped with stone alternatives so the pressure plates are better hidden.

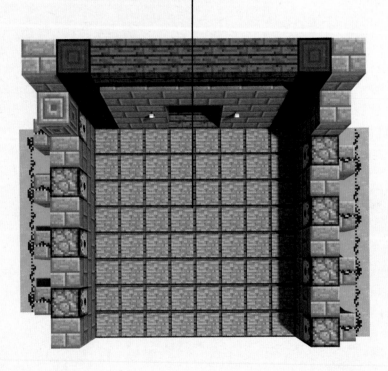

2 Dispenser Layout

When the signal reaches the upper section, it simultaneously powers four dispensers on either side of the trap, sending a flurry of arrows across the room. The dispensers are arranged so that they don't fire directly at the dispensers opposite them. This means that every block of the trap is in range of a dispenser, so there's no escape from the arrows once invaders have made it this far.

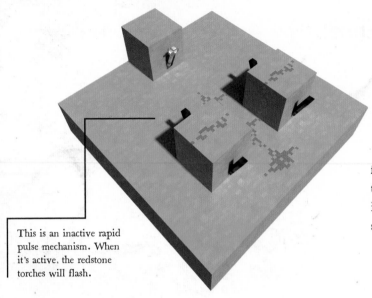

This is an inactive rapid pulse mechanism. When it's active, the redstone torches will flash.

③ Rapid Pulse Mechanism

The mechanism consists of two blocks with redstone running between them, and a redstone torch on the front and back of each block. When a pressure plate is pressed, the signal flows through the redstone grid and repeatedly turns the mechanism off and on, sending intermittent signals through a repeater on each side of the trap towards the upper section.

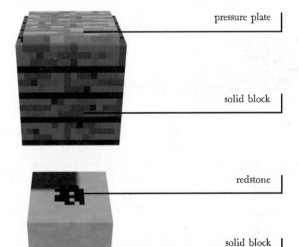

pressure plate

solid block

redstone

solid block

④ Pressure Plates

The entire floor of the arrow gauntlet room is covered in pressure plates, and each pressure plate has a corresponding block of redstone beneath it, in the grid of the lower section. This overall coverage means that every step an intruder takes will start the arrows flying again.

⑤ Variations

To make life really difficult for intruders, the hallway can be made even longer. The redstone grid will need to be continued as far as the pressure plates and arrangement of dispensers extends above. Most importantly, however, a redstone signal can only travel fifteen blocks, so redstone repeaters will need to be placed in four separate places every fifteen blocks. Two of them are shown in the image below, and two more need to be added to the opposite side. Make sure that they are facing in the direction shown, otherwise the circuit will be broken.

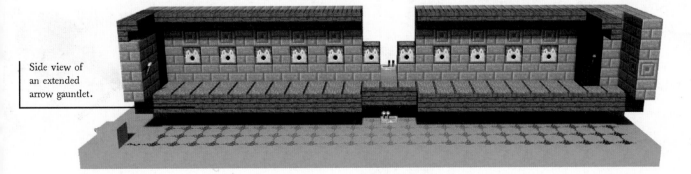

Side view of an extended arrow gauntlet.

ARROW CATAPULT

🕐 **3 HOURS** ❶❷❸❹ **INTERMEDIATE**

Not all of your traps have to exist within your castle walls. If you want to fend off enemies before they even get close to your defences, the arrow catapult is the perfect trap for you. With a few dispensers, TNT and slime blocks, you can rain arrows down on attackers as soon as they appear on the horizon.

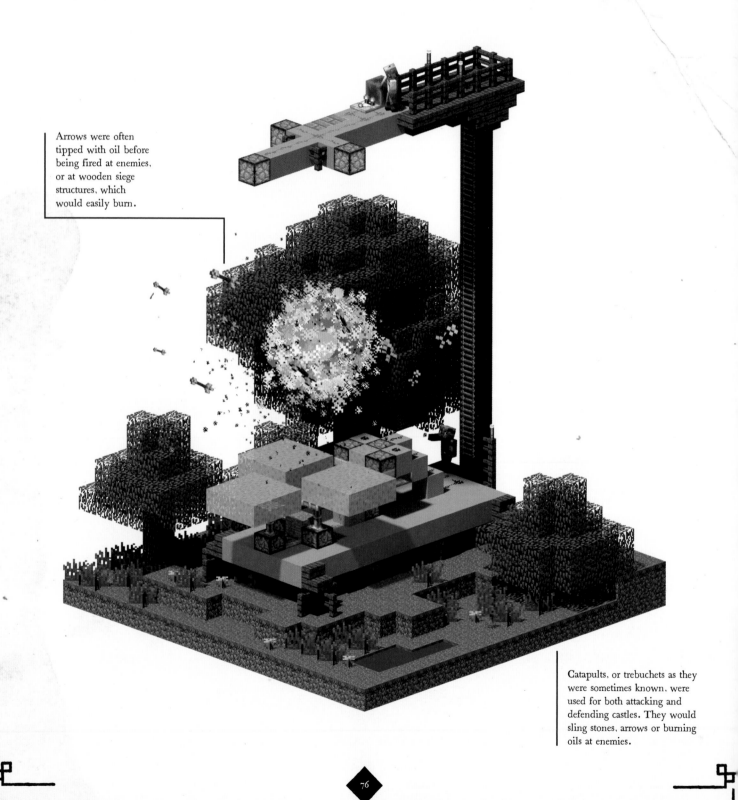

Arrows were often tipped with oil before being fired at enemies, or at wooden siege structures, which would easily burn.

Catapults, or trebuchets as they were sometimes known, were used for both attacking and defending castles. They would sling stones, arrows or burning oils at enemies.

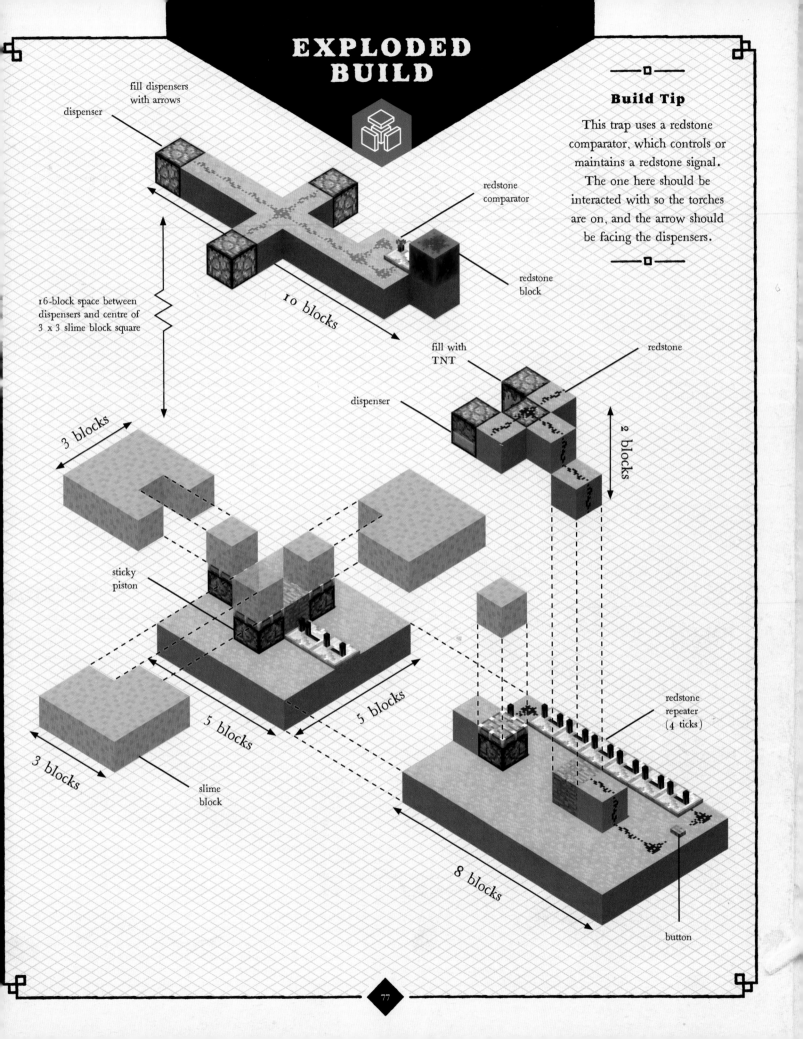

dispenser

fill dispensers
with arrows

Build Tip

This trap uses a redstone
comparator, which controls or
maintains a redstone signal.
The one here should be
interacted with so the torches
are on, and the arrow should
be facing the dispensers.

redstone
comparator

redstone
block

16-block space between
dispensers and centre of
3 x 3 slime block square

10 blocks

fill with
TNT

redstone

dispenser

2 blocks

3 blocks

sticky
piston

5 blocks

redstone
repeater
(4 ticks)

5 blocks

3 blocks

slime
block

8 blocks

button

GETTING IT RIGHT

The catapult is as complicated as it is impressive. It has two main systems, the launcher and the reloader, and needs a long redstone circuit to automate it. But it will be well worth it in the end. Follow these steps to build the ultimate castle defence correctly.

1 TNT Dispenser

The first part of the trap will launch the TNT. When the button is pressed, the dispensers will deploy TNT on a slime block, which is on top of a sticky piston. The button also sends a redstone current to the sticky piston, though it is delayed through a series of redstone repeaters. The piston will push upwards, launching the TNT into the air.

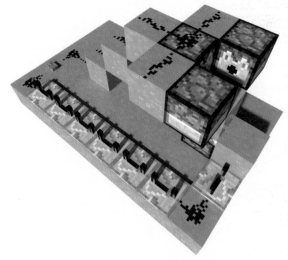

Sticky pistons are under the three highlighted slime blocks.

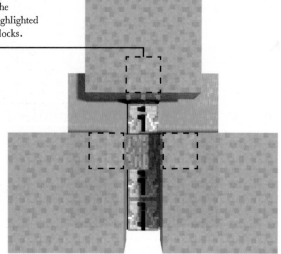

2 Slime Launchers

There are three slime-block launch pads, each with a sticky piston underneath. Launchers are powered by the same button as the TNT dispensers. When they receive the redstone current shortly after the TNT is launched, the pistons will push upwards and launch arrows into the air. The blast from the TNT will then shoot them into the distance.

Make sure the reloading platform is built sixteen blocks above the launchers, otherwise the TNT will destroy the mechanism.

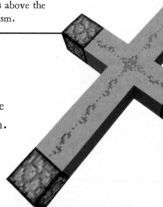

3 Reloading Platform

Once the launching mechanisms are in place they need ammo. A redstone block placed behind a redstone comparator powers the reloading platform. When the comparator is switched on, it powers the dispensers and drops arrows into the launch pads below.

4 Switching to Automated

The reloader and launching mechanisms are now in place, but they can only be controlled manually at the moment. To begin to automate the trap, replace the button controlling the launching mechanism with redstone. Lay redstone from this point, around the trap, until it goes past the front of the launcher. This redstone link will lead to the reload tripwire.

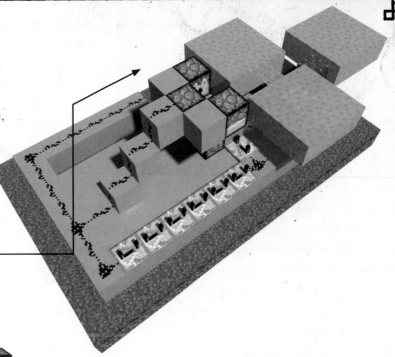

Redstone should go in this direction.

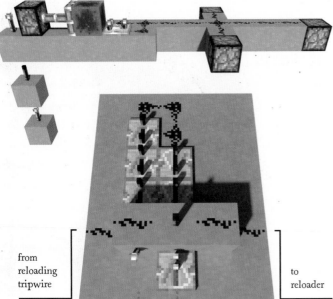

from reloading tripwire

to reloader

5 Automatic Reloader

To automate the reloader, turn the redstone comparator on and move the redstone block back one space. Place a sticky piston behind it so that the redstone can be pushed to power the comparator. Vertical redstone should be used to link the reloader to the ground. From the ground, lay redstone in the same direction as the redstone linking to the launching mechanism. Somewhere along the way, add the breaker circuit shown to the left. This will push the redstone block forward for a short period before turning off again, meaning that only a small number of arrows will be used each time.

6 Tripwire Lengths

Now the redstone links for both mechanisms have been started, they need to be continued to different distances. The reloading circuit link will run furthest – 170 blocks away! At this distance, place a block and attach a tripwire hook to it, then run string parallel to the wall of the castle and attach to another tripwire hook. Do the same for the launch mechanism link, but lay the tripwire 110 blocks away. Now, when someone runs towards the castle, they'll activate both mechanisms and get hit by a volley of arrows around 75 blocks away.

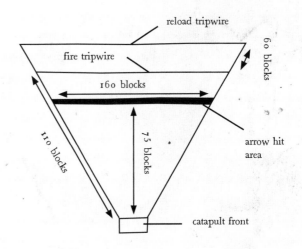

reload tripwire

fire tripwire

60 blocks

160 blocks

110 blocks

75 blocks

arrow hit area

catapult front